UNDERSTANDING THE MYSTERIES OF

KABBALAH

EXPLORING THE ANCIENT ESOTERIC HEART OF JEWISH MYSTICISM

UNDERSTANDING THE MYSTERIES OF

KABBALAH

EXPLORING THE ANCIENT ESOTERIC HEART OF JEWISH MYSTICISM

OFFERS CONCISE AND PRACTICAL INSIGHT INTO THE FOUNDATIONS OF KABBALAH AND EXPLORES HOW IT AIMS TO DEEPEN OUR CONNECTION WITH THE UNIVERSE AND CONTRIBUTE TO THE SEARCH FOR AWARENESS AND TRUE ENLIGHTENMENT

MAGGY WHITEHOUSE

HERMES HOUSE

This edition is published by Hermes House

Hermes House is an imprint of Anness Publishing
Hermes House, 88–89 Blackfriars Road
London SE1 8HA
tel. 020 7401 2077; fax 020 7633 9499
www.annesspublishing.com

© Anness Publishing Ltd 2007

Anness Publishing has a new picture agency outlet for images for publishing, promotions or advertising. Please visit our website www.practicalpictures.com for more information.

ETHICAL TRADING POLICY
Because of our ongoing ecological investment programme, you, as our customer, can have the pleasure and reassurance of knowing that a tree is being cultivated on your behalf to naturally replace the materials used to make the book you are holding. For further information about this scheme, go to: www.annesspublishing.com/trees

All rights reserved. No part of this publication may be reproduced, stored in a retrieval system, or transmitted in any way or by any means, electronic, mechanical, photocopying, recording or otherwise, without the prior written permission of the copyright holder.

A CIP catalogue record for this book is available from the British Library.

Designed and produced for Anness Publishing by
THE BRIDGEWATER BOOK COMPANY LTD.

Publisher Joanna Lorenz
Editorial Director Helen Sudell
Designer Alistair Plumb
Project Manager Polita Caaveiro
Art Director Lisa McCormick
Production Controller Steve Lang

10 9 8 7 6 5 4 3 2

PICTURE ACKNOWLEGEMENTS

Anness Publishing would like to thank the following for kindly supplying photographs for this book: **akg-images London** 11 (tl), 42 (tr), 56 (br), 65 (bl), 89, 95 (b); **Alamy Ltd** 30 (tl), 33 (tr), 36 (bl), 42 (bl), 50 (bc), 54 (tl), 92 (b); **Bridgeman Art Library** 1, 2, 5 (bl), 8 (bl), 12–13, 14 (tr), 16 (tr, bl), 22 (bl), 23 (tr), 27 (tr, br), 29 (cr), 31 (br), 32 (bl), 40 (tl), 43 (br), 44–45, 60 (br), 63 (bl), 64 (tr), 65 (tr), 66 (tl), 67 (tl), 68 (tl), 72–73, 78 (bl); **Corbis** 4, 15 (tl), 24–25, 37 (tr), 41 (tr), 43 (t), 49 (tr), 51, 55 (br), 57 (b), 58 (tl), 74 (tr, bl), 76 (tl), 78 (br), 82 (tr), 84 (tl, br), 85 (br), 86, 88 (tl), 90 (bl), 91 (bl); **Empics** 87 (t), 88 (br); **Fortean Picture Library** 80 (tl); **gettyimages** 39 (tr), 62 (tl), 87 (br), 90 (tr), 91 (tr); **ISFSP International Society for Sephardic Progress** 34 (tr); **iStockphoto** 9 (b), 19 (tr), 50 (tl), 55 (tl), 59 (cr), 60 (tl), 61, 92 (tr), 94 (bl), 95 (tr); **Jupiter Images** 64 (bl); **Maggy Whitehouse** 35 (tl); **Mary Evans Picture Library** 83 (tr); **Picture Desk Ltd** 3, 5 (bc, br), 17 (br), 20 (bl), 21 (tl, br), 22 (tr), 26 (tr), 28 (bl), 30 (br), 31 (t), 34 (bl), 35 (br), 36 (tr), 38 (bl), 48 (tl), 52 (tl), 56 (tl), 68 (br), 75 (tr), 77 (br), 82 (bl), 83 (bl); **Professor James R. Russell** 10 (bl); **Rex Features** 87 (bl); **TopFoto** 6–7, 76 (br), 77 (tl), 79 (tl, cr); **Wellcome Trust Medical Photographic Library** 66 (br); **Z'ev ben Shimon Halevi** 63 (tr), 69 (br), 85 (l), 93 (bl).

Commissioned photography by Suzanne Bosman 9 (tr), 10 (tr), 14 (bl), 15 (cr), 17 (tr), 18 (bl), 20 (tr), 23 (bl), 26 (bl), 27 (cl), 28 (tr), 38 (tr), 40 (bl), 46 (tr), 52 (bl), 57 (tr), 67 (br), 69 (tl), 70 (tl, br), 71 (tr, bl), 79 (cr), 80 (br), 94 (tr).

Particular thanks to Z'ev ben Shimon Halevi 19 (cr), 32 (tr), 41 (cr), 46 (l), 53 (l, r), 58 (r), 63 (tr), 69 (br), 85 (l), 93 (bl).

Every effort has been made to obtain permission to reproduce copyright material, but there may be cases where we have been unable to trace the copyright holder. The publisher will be happy to correct any omissions in future printings.

Images are listed in clockwise order from the top (t = top, c = centre, b = bottom, r = right, l = left, tr = top right etc.).

Contents

PART ONE

INTRODUCTION

Kabbalah is the mystical tradition that underpins Judaism, Islam and Christianity, and it has been a source of wonder, mystery and controversy for more than 2,000 years. Mysticism is the belief that there are truths beyond ordinary human reality or organized religion, and its aim is to help each individual experience direct contact with God. Although Kabbalah is an oral tradition, it uses two diagrams, based on the Jewish structures of the menorah and the Tabernacle. The menorah is a seven-branched candelabrum that modern Kabbalists call the Tree of Life. The Tabernacle was the moveable temple that the Hebrews set up in the wilderness after the exodus from Egypt and is now known as Jacob's Ladder. Kabbalah is taken from the Hebrew word KBLH, which means "receive" or "received wisdom". "Kabbalah" is the spelling used in the Jewish and modern spiritual traditions; however, other groups have spelled it "Cabala" and "Qabalah".

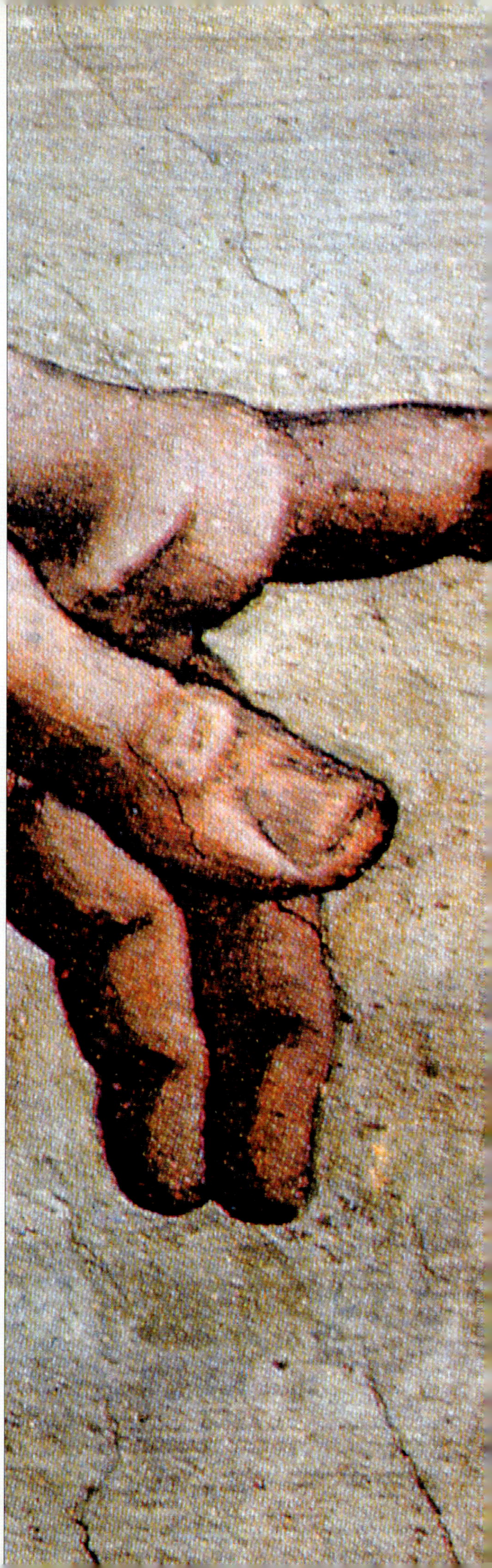

RIGHT The widely-recognized Tree of Life symbol of Kabbalah, overlaid on to the famous detail of the hand of God touching that of Adam from Michelangelo's fresco in the Sistine Chapel, in Rome. The tree has ten principles, or Sefirot (from SPHR, the Hebrew root for circle or sapphire), each representing an aspect of a human being's psyche.

What is Kabbalah?

Kabbalah is a system of understanding life. It is part of the Jewish tradition, and has been nurtured and best understood within Judaism for over 2,000 years. In ages of enlightenment and religious tolerance, such as the Golden Age of Spain in the 11th century, Kabbalah was studied by people of all faiths. However, it is fair to say that most Orthodox Jewish Kabbalists today are uncomfortable with the study of Kabbalah by gentiles. Kabbalah is an oral tradition that uses the diagrams of the Tree of Life and Jacob's Ladder to ensure that continuity and balance are maintained in different traditions of Kabbalistic study.

RIGHT Today the Tree of Life is recognized as the symbol of Kabbalah. Its design depicts the divine, psychological, spiritual and physical make-up of a human – a kind of universal DNA. Kabbalists believe this is the origin of the phrase "God created man in his own image" (Genesis 1:27).

BELOW Humanity has long used symbolism to depict the cosmic and mathematical design of the universe. This image dates back to the 17th century.

Kabbalah is primarily concerned with understanding the relationship between God, humanity and the universe using two diagrams: the Tree of Life and Jacob's Ladder. Unlike written traditions, such as the Bible or the great Kabbalistic books, the oral tradition of Kabbalah is able to evolve relative to the time and place. It retains the structure of Kabbalistic teaching but can adapt to be equally appropriate whether the student is a farmer or an IT specialist. Kabbalah also includes mystical practices such as meditation on the names of God and veneration of what is considered to be the holy power of the Hebrew alphabet, known as *gematria*.

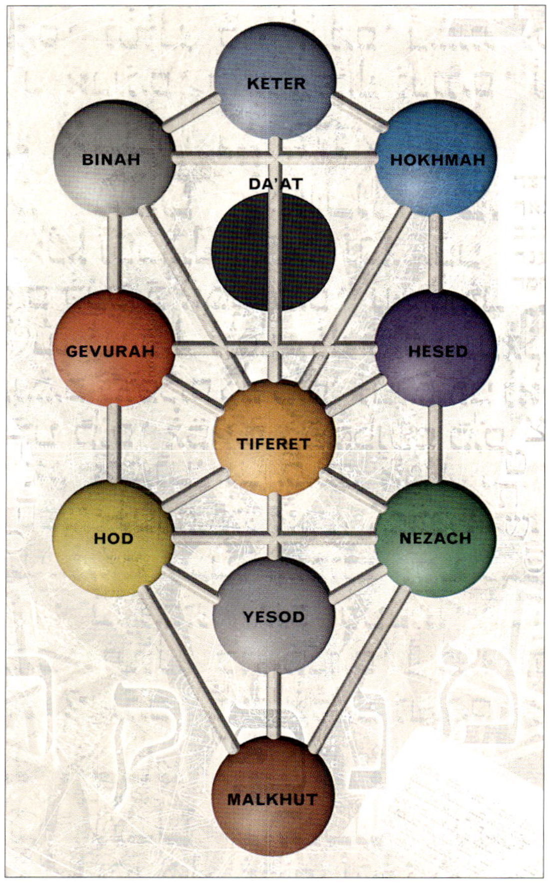

Understanding God

Kabbalah teaches that men and women are children of God and that we are all part of a Divine Plan. When humans are in alignment with the will of God, then they can experience grace or communion with the divine. Grace is a God-given blessing that occurs when a human being is in a state of full consciousness and not just living life on automatic pilot. Kabbalah uses the diagram of the Tree of Life to demonstrate ten principles, called the Sefirot (the plural of Sefira, meaning "circle" or "sapphire"), which represent aspects of the Holy One. Although some modern Kabbalists, including the Los Angeles-based Kabbalah Centre, give more focus to other aspects of Kabbalah, the Tree of Life is the basis for the entire tradition.

UNDERSTANDING THE UNIVERSE

To understand the universe, Kabbalists use the diagram of Jacob's Ladder. This diagram, which only returned to the public domain in the 1970s after 400 years of being hidden deep within Kabbalistic tradition, is based on the design of the tabernacle – the place of worship created by God and given to Moses, as related in the Book of Exodus. It was also later used for the Jewish Temple. At a cosmic level, Jacob's Ladder is used as a map of the universe, demonstrating the invisible laws that establish and maintain the cycles of the stars, planets and nature.

Kabbalistic teaching maintains that the creation of the universe occurred at four levels, each one representing an element. These are: Azilut, the divine level, represented by fire; Beriah, the spiritual level, represented by air; Yezirah, the psychological plane of the soul, represented by water; and Asiyyah, the physical world, represented by earth (physical reality). All these elements are present throughout the universe, and they obey Cosmic Law, or the Law of Karma (cause and effect). This is most often described in the Western world as "the law of attraction"or "what goes around comes around", or through Isaac Newton's Third Law of Motion: "for every action there is an equal and opposite reaction". Kabbalah teaches that, as children of God, our thoughts, words and actions all invoke this karmic law. No blame is attached to this; the universe is impartial and non-judgemental; it just works according to the Law.

ABOVE In the Book of Genesis, Jacob dreamt that God spoke to him from the divine world at the top of a ladder reaching from Earth to heaven. Angels ascended and descended on this ladder, which became the basis of the Kabbalistic diagram of the four worlds of existence.

UNDERSTANDING HUMANITY

The diagram of the Tree of Life is the Kabbalistic explanation for the phrase "and God made man in his own image" (Genesis 1:27). Kabbalah teaches that the Tree of Life has ten aspects, the Sefirot, which represent the ten aspects of God. As each human being is made in the image of God, each human also contains ten aspects of divinity. How these aspects balance within each person depends on their upbringing, environment, astrological blueprint and whether they have the self-discipline to practise the principle of free will. The structure of the Tree of Life offers a "design for living" that can be used by people of all faiths to assess how to achieve a balanced life. One of the reasons why Kabbalah is often perceived as being difficult or dangerous by those who have not studied it is because it requires discipline, both in learning the principles and in applying them to everyday life.

BELOW Light and fire are the Kabbalistic symbols for divinity. The universe and the diversity of life within it springs from the "endless light" of God. The human self is one of a myriad of sparks in the great design of life.

THE CREATION

ACCORDING TO LEGEND, BEING ABSOLUTE AND ALL, THE HOLY ONE WAS COMPLETE BUT, EVEN SO, IT HELD A DESIRE TO EXPERIENCE ITSELF AS IF FROM OUTSIDE, AND THIS WAS WHY THE CREATION CAME INTO BEING. THE DIVINE PLAN IS THEREFORE FOR "GOD TO BEHOLD GOD". THIS GOD IS KNOWN AS *AYIN* – "NOTHINGNESS" IN HEBREW – BECAUSE IT IS BEYOND EXISTENCE AND IS INCOMPREHENSIBLE TO HUMANS. TO BEGIN THE PROCESS OF EXISTENCE, AYIN (THE TRANSCENDENT) WITHDREW AN ASPECT OF ITSELF – GOD THE IMMANENT, KNOWN AS *AYIN SOF*, THE ABSOLUTE ALL – IN ORDER TO CREATE A SPACE WITHIN ITSELF. THIS SPACE IS KNOWN AS *ZIMZUM*. AROUND THIS SPACE WAS *AYIN SOF OR*, THE ENDLESS LIGHT, FROM WHICH CAME THE EMANATION THAT BEGAN THE UNFOLDING OF CREATION.

RIGHT Gustave Doré's painting shows God commanding light on the first day of creation. Although the second commandment forbids the creation of a "graven image" of divinity, the idea of God as an old man supervising the universe has been propagated by Christianity.

For modern Kabbalists an easier interpretation of the Creation might be to regard the Transcendent as the parent, the Immanent as the womb, and the Endless Light as the lining of the womb, where life can begin.

THE REASON FOR CREATION

The desire of God to behold God is the foundation of the perennial human wish to give birth. Humanity is the "divine baby", and Kabbalah teaches that each one of us is one cell in the body of a great Being of Light, Adam Kadmon. Only through this process of creation could God

experience the diversity of thought, feeling and movement that is possible in life. Kabbalah teaches that the goal for humanity is to perfect itself; to learn to live life as great beings of all faiths have done without fear or hatred. To a Kabbalist, Jesus of Nazareth or the Buddha would be beings who had developed themselves to the point of perfection over many lives.

RIGHT Ayin, the Absolute Nothing and Ayin Sof, the Absolute All, are the sources of creation. Here, Z'ev Ben Shimon Halevi's illustration shows the will of the Divine manifesting in the Ayin Sof Or – the endless light – ten attributes of fire, contained within the cosmic womb.

THE LIGHTNING FLASH

Kabbalah teaches that the process of creation required the balancing of two pillars. Without something to restrain its impulse, light would be without purpose. Everything that starts must have a stopping point: a kettle will boil dry if it is not switched off when the correct temperature has been

reached. Similarly, there must be a stopping point in every race, or there could be no winner.

Each new impulse of creation had to be balanced and stabilized as light flowed into the void created by God. In the same way, an embryo grows and then stabilizes that growth through developing bone and muscle structure. The Lightning Flash, which emanates from the Endless Light, begins at Keter, the Crown, flowing first to the active Sefira of Hokhmah (Wisdom), then across to the passive Sefira of Binah (Understanding), where that growth is stabilized. It then flows across the abyss of Da'at to the active Sefira of Hesed (Mercy) and back to the passive Sefira of Gevurah (Judgement) for the new growth to consolidate. The place of the abyss, (Da'at) in a human or animal life, is the moment when an embryo either lodges in the lining of the womb or spontaneously aborts. In the same way, an idea can thrive or be lost.

From Gevurah, the Lightning Flash passes to Tiferet (Beauty), where quickening takes place, before moving to the active principle of Nezach (Eternity) for rapid brain and cell growth, and back to passive Hod (Reverberation) for the consolidation of muscle and fat. From there it balances itself in Yesod (Foundation) before becoming manifest – or born – in Malkhut (Kingdom). The Lightning Flash flows down through the four worlds of Jacob's Ladder from fire, through air and water to earth, becoming slower and more dense at each stage.

ADAM KADMON, THE DIVINE HUMAN

Hebrew for primordial man, Adam Kadmon is the starting point for the generation of humanity. It is a concept of the perfect human being – a being of light. Every single human soul is said to be one cell in Adam Kadmon, leading to the Kabbalistic belief that every single human will become perfect in order for the "divine baby" to be born. Each human is equally important in the Holy One's plan of creation. Adam Kadmon is neither masculine nor feminine and has no race or religion.

References to this divine figure are found in many early Kabbalistic works as the origin of the idea that man is made in God's image. According to legend, each human soul comes from a different aspect of Adam Kadmon, and a soul may have a specific destiny as a soldier, a nurse or an inventor. Adam Kadmon exists in Azilut, the divine world of fire.

LEFT Probably the best-known image of God and creation is Kabbalist and mystic William Blake's *The Ancient of Days*, which shows the great cosmic design in process.

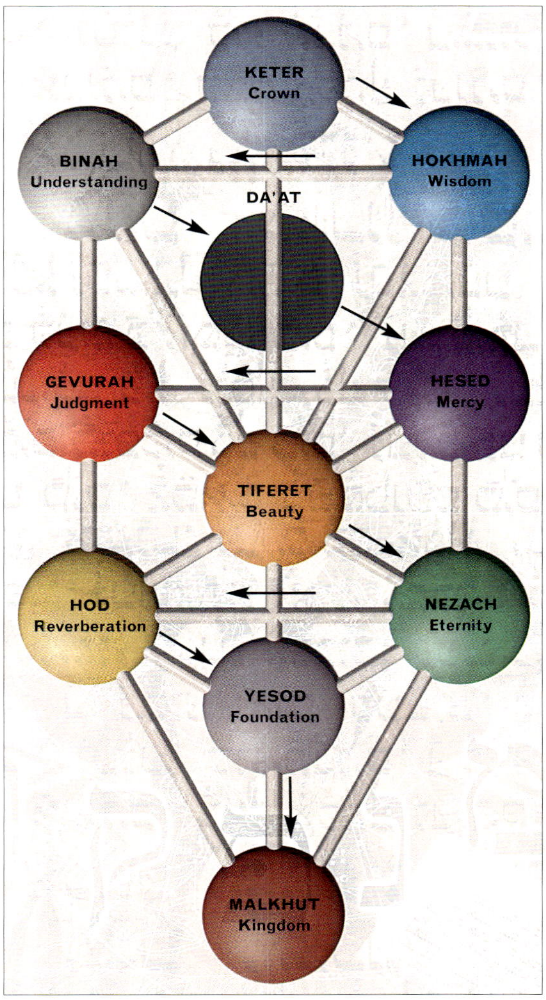

LEFT The Lightning Flash follows the path of the Sefirot down the Tree of Life. If you trace the sequence on a diagram of the Tree, you will see that it has the zigzag shape of a lightning flash. This sequence describes the process of creation, beginning with the unknown, unmanifest, hidden God – the creator in Keter – and follows it through ten distinct stages to a change in the material world – the created in Malkhut. It can be used to describe any change, from lighting a match to walking the dog.

PART TWO

KABBALAH IN THE ANCIENT WORLD

Kabbalah is the story of humanity, and it runs parallel to the Jewish written teachings throughout the Old Testament. The word 'Kabbalah' was not the name of a tradition in Old Testament times, but simply a description of what happened when a wise man or woman was able to perceive and transmit wisdom directly from God. Kabbalah means "to receive", and the wise person became known as a Kabbalist because he or she received the word of God. The majority of people did not read or write, so they learned their faith through oral story-telling. These stories would have four different kinds of interpretation – literal, psychological, spiritual and mystical. Kabbalah began on the day that the first human being told a story. According to legend, it was first given to Adam and Eve when they left Eden, in order to help their descendents return to paradise.

RIGHT The Temple is always depicted as having four specific areas representing the Kabbalistic four worlds. This 15th-century woodcut of the walled city of Jerusalem depicts the city as having been built in four sections, with the whole Temple complex representing Azilut, the divine world.

TEPLVM·SALOMOIS·

Expulsion from Eden

The idea that humanity sinned against God and was expelled from paradise to live a life of strife and suffering is part of most faiths. The expulsion from Eden has long been used to demonstrate humanity's disobedience of God's will and to describe woman as a temptress. Kabbalistic interpretations differ from the written religious ones in that the "fall" is seen as a necessary, expected part of humanity's evolution. Eden is not considered to be a physical place but a realm of the soul that must be left in order to incarnate on Earth and, from there, begin the process of returning to God. The Book of Raziel, which was supposedly given to Adam and Eve when they left Eden, forms the basis of Kabbalistic teaching.

RIGHT The Tree of Life, represented here and in many works of art, is central to the teachings of Kabbalah. It offers insights into the world around us and the world within us.

BELOW It was Eve who made the first ever free-will decision in picking and eating the apple from the Tree of Knowledge of Good and Evil. So began the path of human development in which every single choice we make in life is just as important as that first one.

Adam and Eve, the first created man and woman in the biblical story of Genesis, lived in the Garden of Eden, a paradise where there was no death. They were allowed to eat from any of the trees and plants – apart from one, the Tree of Knowledge of Good and Evil. Eve was tempted by a serpent (usually depicted as Satan) to eat the fruit of the tree, which she did. Adam also ate it. They then became aware of the possibility of opposites; of their own sexuality and of their nakedness, and covered their sexual organs. When God discovered what they had done, he banished them from Eden to a life of toil, reproduction, pain and death.

KABBALISTIC INTERPRETATION

It is the belief of Kabbalists that Adam and Eve, the first souls to descend from the divine Adam Kadmon, existed only in the psychological world known as Yezirah – a realm of the psyche; a place of images and dreams but not physical reality. While they existed in this realm of paradise, no

growth or experience could happen, and no choices could be made, as they had no concept of duality – the ability to choose between options. Choice, the essence of free will, was required for Adam Kadmon, the divine baby, to "quicken".

In modern day parlance, the injunction not to eat from the Tree of Knowledge was "a set-up", so that the four great journeys of humanity could begin and God could behold God. Although she disobeyed God's command, it was Eve's decision to break the rules that gave humanity its first taste of the idea of choice and its consequences.

THE CONCEPT OF CHOICE

Once Adam and Eve had made the choice, and their eyes were opened to the fact that everything else in life would require further choice, they were ready to descend from paradise to the physical world, where decisions have to be made every day. This is the meaning of the phrase "Unto Adam also and to his wife did the Lord God make coats of skins, and clothed them" (Genesis 3:21). The couple became physically human in their own skin as they were born into the physical world of the Earth.

This story is intended to tell us that all our choices in life matter, and that the good and bad things that befall us every day are of our own creation, not random events from an uncaring universe.

According to the Book of Genesis, there was a another important tree in the Garden of Eden – the Tree of Life. When Adam and Eve were expelled, God "placed at the east of the Garden of Eden, cherubim, and a flaming sword which turned every way, to keep the way of the tree of life" (Genesis 3:24). Kabbalah sees the Tree of Life as the route back home to Eden. There is also a legend that when Adam and Eve went down into the lower worlds after eating from the Tree of Knowledge, Eve took a twig and planted it outside Eden to remind them of the importance of making the right choices. A staff was cut from Eve's tree and passed down through generations until it was given to Moses by his wife Zipporah. It was called the "staff of sapphires". The Hebrew root word for sapphire is SPHR, the same as for "Sefira".

LEFT It is humanity's longing to return to the paradise of the Garden of Eden that fuels the search for spiritual inspiration. This 16th-century image of the *Garden of Earthly Delights* shows God, humanity and animals living together in peace.

BELOW Adam and Eve leaving Eden – and all that they had ever known. This is the same as setting out on a personal spiritual journey. Spiritual growth is rarely comfortable and never convenient, but there is angelic help to guide us on our journey.

THE BOOK OF RAZIEL

Legend states that when Adam and Eve left the Garden of Eden they were given the Book of Raziel, which was a guide to how to find their way back home to the spiritual realm. This guide has formed the basis of Kabbalistic teaching for 2,000 years. The name Raziel means "secrets of God", and Raziel is the archangel said to be in charge of this sacred knowledge, which was passed down from spiritual leader to spiritual leader over generations. A version of the Book of Raziel, printed in Amsterdam in 1701, contains details of amulets and incantations, but generally it is believed to be an oral tradition inspired by the Tree of Life.

GENESIS AND THE TORAH

THE TORAH, THE FIRST FIVE BOOKS OF THE HEBREW BIBLE, TELLS THE STORY OF HUMANITY'S FIRST EFFORTS TO DEAL WITH LIFE, DEATH, RELATIONSHIPS, SLAVERY AND FAITH. IN A LIVING TRADITION SUCH AS KABBALAH, THERE ARE TALES TO BE TOLD BEHIND THE WRITTEN STORIES AND, IN THE 1ST CENTURY CE, MANY OF THEM WERE WRITTEN DOWN IN THE TALMUD, HAGGADAH AND MIDRASH, ALL COMMENTARIES ON THE TORAH. AS WELL AS THE TEN COMMANDMENTS, ORTHODOX JEWS OBEY 613 LAWS AS LAID DOWN BY THE TORAH. HOWEVER, INTERPRETATION OF THESE LAWS VARIES ACCORDING TO DIFFERENT SCHOOLS OF TALMUDIC THOUGHT, AND ALL ARE SECONDARY TO THE COMMANDMENT TO PRESERVE LIFE.

ABRAHAM AND SARAH

Better known to us today as Abraham and Sarah, Abram and Sarai were the first biblical patriarch and matriarch – the wise people of the Torah. In Kabbalistic legend, they were initiated into the secret teaching from the Book of Raziel by Melchizedek, King of Salem, "and Melchizedek king of Salem brought forth bread and wine: and he was the priest of the most high God" (Genesis 14:7). This is the first reference to what became the basis for the Sabbath Eve service in Judaism and later the Christian Holy Communion.

RIGHT While the Bible has been a source of inspiration, it is also the source of much fundamentalist belief. The Christian mystic William Blake's poem, *The Divine Image* is a plea for religious tolerance: "And all must love the human form, In Heathen, Turk, or Jew; Where Mercy, Love, & Pity dwell, There God is dwelling too".

RIGHT Job, Isaiah, Jeremiah, Solomon, Moses, Ezekiel, David and Enoch, all prominent Old Testament characters, are depicted in this 14th-century Italian fresco. The women of the Old Testament have equally important stories to tell, but the feminine is often hidden in religious texts. Kabbalistically, this is to encourage spiritual seekers to investigate the truth for themselves rather than just listening to the well-told stories.

The story is told in Genesis of how Abram and Sarai travelled to Egypt, where the pharaoh was so taken with Sarai's beauty that he took her for his harem. However, God struck the pharaoh with plagues, so he set her free. Kabbalah teaches that it was the Shekhinah – the feminine aspect of God – acting through Sarai that struck the pharaoh and that it is also this divine feminine aspect that is called down into the home at the striking of the lights for the inauguration of the Sabbath on a Friday night. In Midrash, Genesis Rabbah (60), a commentary on the Torah, it states that the light went out in Abram's tent when Sarah died until their son Isaac married. "When she died, the lamp ceased; and when Rebekah came, the lamp returned."

ENOCH – THE FIRST REALIZED MAN

Enoch merits only four verses in the Book of Genesis (5:21-24). He lived, according to the Hebrew Bible, for 365 years and "walked with God; then he was no more for God took him". This is taken to mean that Enoch ascended bodily into heaven. To Kabbalists, Enoch is the first man to have completed the four journeys and become fully integrated into Adam Kadmon. He is the only known man to become an archangelic being – known as Metatron – although he is placed closer to God than the archangels themselves. The Book of Enoch has been known as an important esoteric text for many centuries and was quoted by some of the early Christian Church Fathers. However, the original Aramaic version of it had been lost for many centuries, until the discovery of the Dead Sea Scrolls at Qumran, Israel, in 1947.

SHEKHINAH (THE FEMININE OF GOD)

The word Shekhinah is not found in the Bible, and the word is generally believed to have first been used by scholars after the Old and New Testaments were written. However, the idea of the presence of God is referred to throughout the Scriptures by the word *shakan*, a feminine Hebrew verb that means "to dwell". Shekhinah is the development of this verb into a noun, which is also feminine. In both the Hebrew Bible and the Qumran Isaiah Scroll, the pronouns referring to God comforting his people with his presence are feminine. In Kabbalistic teaching, Shekhinah is said to be the aspect of God that gives birth to souls and receives them back after death.

MARRIAGE AS A SACRAMENT

The Jewish belief that marriage is a command from God is based on Genesis 2:18, where God says, "it is not good that a man should be alone; I shall make a help-meet (*ayzer* – one who nurtures) for him... therefore shall a man leave his father and mother and shall cleave to his wife, and they shall become one flesh." A rabbi in biblical times (and an Orthodox Jewish rabbi today) had to be married. The "conjugal life" section of the Kabbalistic book the Zohar states that man has two female partners, with the Shekhinah, as the Supernal Mother, alongside the man's earthly wife. When a man is away from his female partner, God takes over the part of the wife, as well as that of the higher feminine, so that the man is never alone. Shekhinah is now very popular among women who are seeking "Goddess energy", but to a Kabbalist it is vital to keep the eternal balance between masculine and feminine, and to understand that God itself, the Holy One, is beyond sexual definition.

ABOVE This 17th-century wedding ceremony of two Portuguese Jews shows the bridegroom breaking a glass underfoot. This is an expression of sadness at the destruction of the Temple in Jerusalem and is carried out at all Jewish weddings. The canopy (*Chuppah*) overhead symbolizes the tent of Abram and Sarai, the first Patriarch and Matriarch, who had their tent open on all sides to welcome friends and relatives in unconditional hospitality.

LEFT Abraham is blessed with bread and wine by the high priest and king of Salem, Melchizedek, as he is initiated into the mysteries of the inner teaching of Kabbalah (Genesis 14:18). This initiation ceremony is repeated by Jesus of Nazareth for his disciples at the Last Supper and forms the basis for the Christian Communion service. Jesus himself is confirmed as a high priest after the Order of Melchizedek in Hebrews 5:10.

MOSES AND THE MENORAH

THE GREAT KABBALISTIC DESIGNS OF THE TREE OF LIFE AND JACOB'S LADDER ARE FIRST REFERRED TO IN THE BOOK OF EXODUS, WHEN THE ISRAELITES ARE TRAVELLING IN THE DESERT, HAVING ESCAPED FROM SLAVERY IN EGYPT. THIS WAS THE THIRD TIME THAT KABBALAH WAS GIVEN. SINCE, IN THOSE DAYS, FEW PEOPLE READ OR WROTE, AND AS THE ISRAELITES WERE A WANDERING NATION IN THE DESERT, THEY NEEDED SOME KIND OF BASIS FOR THEIR FAITH THAT WAS BOTH EASY TO UNDERSTAND AND TO TRANSPORT ON THEIR JOURNEY TO THE PROMISED LAND. GOD COMMANDED MOSES TO BUILD THE SEVEN-BRANCHED CANDELABRUM KNOWN AS THE MENORAH AND THE TABERNACLE WHERE IT WOULD RESIDE. THE TABERNACLE LATER BECAME THE SACRED JEWISH TEMPLE IN JERUSALEM. ALSO IN THE TABERNACLE WAS THE ARK OF THE COVENANT, WHERE THE TABLETS CONTAINING THE TEN COMMANDMENTS WERE KEPT.

RIGHT Moses presenting the Ten Commandments carved in stone to the Israelites. Moses is often depicted in art with two horns, or two rays of light emanating from his head. The idea of horns originated in the 4th century with St Jerome, who translated the Bible from Hebrew and Greek into Latin. He mistakenly translated the Hebrew word *karnu* (ray) into the Latin *cornuta* (horned). The original Hebrew referred to Moses' face being illuminated by rays of the light of God.

RIGHT The erection of the tabernacle – the moving temple – by the Israelites in the wilderness. The precise instructions for the temple are in Exodus chapters 25 and 26, with instructions for the high priest's clothing in chapter 27. This design was followed faithfully for the First Temple in Jerusalem (in the time of Solomon) and the Second Temple, built by Herod the Great 2000 years ago. The site of the Temple in Jerusalem is now a sacred place for Islam and is known as the Dome of the Rock.

The design of the menorah represents the Tree of Life and, repeated four times to represent the four worlds of creation, it creates Jacob's Ladder, the design of the Tabernacle, or Jewish Temple.

THE MENORAH

One of the oldest symbols of the Jewish faith, the menorah was a seven-branched candelabrum made entirely from one piece of gold. The gold came from jewellery and treasure that the Israelites had been able to take with them when they left Egypt. Exodus 25:32-36 gives the entire instruction: "And six branches shall come out of the sides of it; three branches of the candlestick out of the one side, and three branches of the candlestick out of the other side: Three bowls made like unto almonds, with a knop and a flower in one branch; and three bowls made like almonds in the other branch, with a knop and a flower: so in the six branches that come out of the candlestick. And in the candlestick shall be four bowls made like unto almonds, with their knops and their flowers. And there shall be a knop under two branches of the same, and a knop under two branches of the same, and a knop under two branches of the same, according to the six branches that proceed out of the candlestick. Their knops and their branches shall be of the same: all it shall be one beaten work of pure gold." All the bowls, knops, branches and flowers were later translated into the four worlds (see box), the Sefirot and the pathways of the Tree of Life.

THE DESIGN OF THE TABERNACLE

Instructions for the Tabernacle, the moveable temple of the Israelites, are detailed in chapters 25–40 in Exodus. This complex creation included the building of the Ark of the Covenant, and there were specific instructions as to how many curtains should be made, and what they were to be made from; the types of wood that could be used; and the creation of four areas that were designated for different uses. The outer court was screened from the outside by white linen curtains approximately 46m (150ft) long, 23m (75ft) wide, and 2.3m (7½ft) tall. Inside was a burnt-offering altar for sacrifices, a "laver" (a place for washing – nowadays Jews use a ritual bath called a *mikvah*), and the Holy of Holies – the most sacred place, where the Ark was kept and which only the high priest could enter. Solomon's Temple and the Second Temple, built by Herod the Great before the time of Jesus, were constructed on the same design.

THE TEN COMMANDMENTS

As revealed in the Book of Exodus, the Ten Commandments that were given to Moses formed the basis of the laws that the Israelites were to obey. Each one relates to one of the ten Sefirot on the menorah and the Kabbalistic Tree of Life. The first three commandments, all dealing with humanity's relationship with God are at Keter, Hokhmah and Binah, which are known as the Supernal Triad. The seven Sefirot below them are concerned with everyday life and the choices that we have to make.

According to Kabbalistic legend, Moses was given the commandments twice, the first time in an esoteric form as sacred advice for living. The first commandments were written on sapphire but, when the Israelites proved they were not ready for those, a second list of commandments was issued in stone. The Sefirot on the menorah and the Tree of Life are intended to be indications of the original commandments.

THE FOUR WORLDS

The four worlds of creation are depicted both in the menorah, which has four "cups", and in the Tabernacle with its four courts. In the temples that were later built, these could be seen in the Court of the Gentiles (the physical world, known as Asiyyah), the Court of the Men (the spiritual world, known as Beriah), the Court of the Women (the psychological world, known as Yezirah), and the Sanctuary (the divine world, known as Azilut).

ABOVE The menorah is a seven-branched candelabrum to be lit by oil in the Tabernacle and the Jewish Temple in Jerusalem. The Menorah is one of the oldest symbols of the Jewish people. It is said to symbolize the burning bush, as seen by Moses on Mount Sinai.

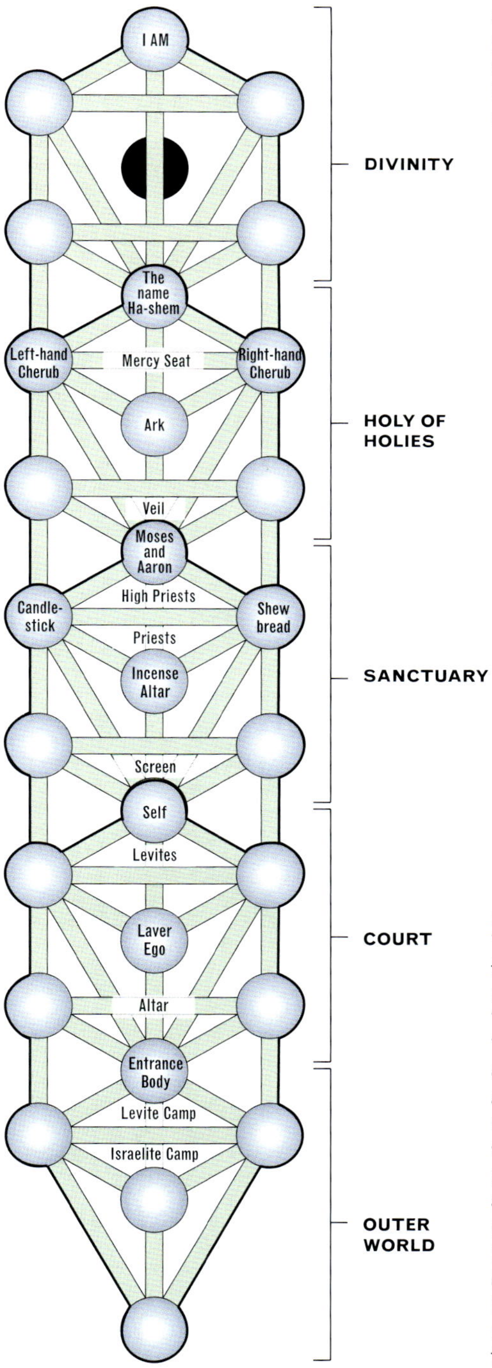

LEFT The design of the Temple is the basis for the Kabbalistic diagram of Jacob's Ladder. The instructions for the Temple included the colours red, purple, blue and linen (white), which represent the four worlds of the physical, psychological, spiritual and divine. Only the high priest was allowed in the heart of the Temple, known as the Holy of Holies, where the menorah and the Ark of the Covenant were placed.

Chariot Riders

THE KABBALISTIC TRADITION HAD NO NAME IN EARLY BIBLICAL TIMES. THE WRITING OF THE OLD TESTAMENT BOOK OF EZEKIEL CHANGED THIS, HOWEVER, AS IT DESCRIBED A KABBALISTIC VISION OF ASCENSION TO THE HIGHER WORLDS. THIS PRACTICE BECAME KNOWN AS MERKABAH – FROM 'HAMERKAVAH', THE HEBREW WORD FOR CHARIOT – AND IT IS BASED ON THE VISION OF THE PROPHET EZEKIEL. THE CHARIOT PASSAGE IN THE BOOK OF EZEKIEL IS CONSIDERED TO BE SO MYSTERIOUS THAT THE ANCIENT SAGES WERE RELUCTANT TO STUDY OR TEACH IT. STUDENTS OF THE RABBIS WERE WARNED TO AVOID THE PASSAGE DUE TO ITS IMMENSE HOLINESS. STUDENTS OF KABBALAH STUDY EZEKIEL'S VISION THROUGH MEDITATION, AND THEY ARE ONLY TAUGHT THE TECHNIQUES FOR "RIDING THE CHARIOT" WHEN THEY ARE CONSIDERED MATURE ENOUGH TO BE ABLE TO HANDLE THE KNOWLEDGE OF DIRECT EXPERIENCE OF THE DIVINE.

RIGHT Ezekiel's vision depicted "the appearance of the likeness of the glory of the Lord" in the form of a man who spoke to him, calling him "son of Man" (Ezekiel 2:1). This appellation is reserved for those who have direct contact with God, such as Jesus of Nazareth.

The Old Testament tells us that when the prophet Ezekiel was a 30-year-old priest beginning a divinely-ordained ministry, he had a spectacular vision that led to direct contact with the divine presence. This took place after the Israelite nation had been conquered and taken captive by the Babylonians in the 6th century BCE.

EZEKIEL'S VISION

The priest saw a huge storm cloud approaching from the north with a glowing light in the centre that resembled a bright amber-like metal.

RIGHT Ezekiel's vision, believed to date back to the 6th century BCE, is the basis for the Kabbalistic meditative practice of "chariot-riding", known as Merkabah. The vision included the origin of the four holy creatures – ox, lion, eagle and man – which represent the four fixed astrological signs of Taurus, Leo, Scorpio and Aquarius, and the four worlds of Asiyyah, Yezirah, Beriah and Azilut.

Within it was the "throne chariot of God" (I Chronicles 28:18). This was carried by four creatures, partly human, each with four faces, four wings, human-looking hands and calf's feet. The faces on each were the four holy creatures of ox, lion, eagle and man. A later chapter in the Book of Ezekiel identifies the creatures as the angels known as cherubim, who guard the Ark of the Covenant (Exodus 25:17-22 and Numbers 7:89). The Ark and, later, the Temple were symbolic representations of God's heavenly throne. Below the cherubim were

LEFT A mosaic apse in the 9th-century Palatine chapel in Germigny des Près, France, showing the Ark of the Covenant. The two angels on the lid of the sacred ark are said to be cherubim. According to legend, the energy of a cherub is greater than a star such as the Sun. Cherubim comprise one of the highest ranks of the archangels.

wheels of a bright, shining yellow-green. The wheels intersected each other at right angles, enabling the chariot to move in all directions without turning, just as the faces of the four holy creatures were able to gaze in all directions at once. The rims of the chariot's wheels were full of eyes.

Biblical commentaries emphasize that Ezekiel's vision is not meant to be taken literally as the definitive image of God. The chariot and angels are analogies of one of the many ways in which God can become manifest in the world. The throne on wheels image is similar to the religious imagery of several other cultures and mythologies, including the sun-gods of Egyptian and Hellenic cultures.

MYSTICAL CHARIOT RIDERS

Since the 3rd century CE there has been written evidence of Kabbalistic sages and mystics who performed a mystical process known as "riding the chariot", based on Ezekiel's vision. Chariot riders aimed to ascend to the divine throne through a series of meditations and rituals. Each of these would lift the mystic's consciousness higher through seven levels known as the Seven Heavens, where they would view great and awe-inspiring sights.

In the New Testament, St Paul writes of a mystic who ascended to the "third heaven" and heard and saw unutterable mysteries (II Corinthians 12:2). The prophet Muhammad's midnight ride to heaven on El-Buraq is also similar to the imagery of Merkabah mysticism. The Book of Revelation is almost certainly a Merkabah vision, with its account of apocalyptic sights, cosmology, celestial hosts and heaven, with revelations of the hidden glory of the divine, including many references to seven levels, including seven seals, seven angels of seven churches and seven trumpets.

In modern days, Merkabah chariot riding is still practised by experienced mystics, but it is only attempted in the company of fellow Kabbalists who can support the aspirant and ensure that he or she is kept safe on the inner journey. While attempting a meditation of this intensity the aspirant must be simultaneously grounded and inspired. The effect of such deep inner work can be the equivalent of taking a mind-expanding drug and can have similar after-effects unless achieved consciously and after due study and preparation.

LEFT The four holy creatures of the vision were adopted by the Christian faith, and they represent the Gospels of Matthew (ox), Mark (lion), Luke (eagle) and John (man). They also appear in the New Testament Book of Revelation, 4:7: "And the first beast was like a lion, and the second beast like a calf, and the third beast had a face as a man, and the fourth beast was like a flying eagle."

THE FOUR WISE MEN WHO ASCENDED THE HEAVENS

There is a legend of four wise men who attempted the ascent through the heavens by meditating on the divine name. The men were Ben Azzai, Ben Zoma, Elisha ben Avuya and Rabbi Akiva. Ben Azzai gazed at the divine presence and died. Ben Zoma gazed and lost his sanity. Ben Avuya lost his faith and became a heretic. Rabbi Akiva entered in peace and left in peace. The story is meant to demonstrate the importance of being balanced and wise before attempting inner, mystical work. Many people in the modern-day New Age movement neglect inner work and attempt to attain too much spiritual knowledge too soon.

THE NEW TESTAMENT

IT IS UNDERSTANDABLY OFFENSIVE TO MANY JEWISH KABBALISTS THAT JESUS OF NAZARETH IS SOMETIMES REFERRED TO AS A KABBALIST. JESUS IS CONSIDERED A CHRISTIAN RATHER THAN A JEW; FURTHER, WITHIN JUDAISM, CHRISTIANITY IS CONSIDERED TO HAVE STOLEN MUCH OF JEWISH THOUGHT. HOWEVER, THERE IS EVIDENCE IN THE GOSPELS THAT JESUS OF NAZARETH UNDERSTOOD THE JEWISH MYSTICAL TRADITION. THE "LORD'S PRAYER", FOR EXAMPLE, FITS ON TO BOTH THE TREE OF LIFE AND JACOB'S LADDER. EVEN CLEARER EVIDENCE IS IN THE CHOICE OF THE FOUR GOSPELS OF MATTHEW, MARK, LUKE AND JOHN, WHICH TELL THE STORY OF JESUS' LIFE AND TEACHINGS. THESE APPEAR TO SHOW KABBALISTIC KNOWLEDGE OF THE FOUR WORLDS AND THE LEVELS OF UNDERSTANDING OF HUMANITY. THE MAJORITY OF NON-JEWISH KABBALISTS STUDYING IN THE 21ST CENTURY BELIEVE JESUS TO HAVE BEEN A GREAT TEACHER OF MYSTICAL TRUTH RATHER THAN THE MESSIAH.

RIGHT St John writing *In principio erat verbum* (in the beginning was the Word), from an 11th-century French bible.

In Jesus' day there were three main groups of Jewish teaching. The Sadducees, the Pharisees (including the Scribes) and the Essenes.

The Sadducees followed the written law of the Torah to the letter and did not believe in life after death. The Essenes thought that the Jewish Temple was corrupt and lived lives of worship both in the towns of Judea and in separate communities. They did not carry out animal sacrifices and developed their own line of teaching that was both an oral and a written tradition. The Pharisees took the middle ground; honouring the Torah and the Temple but also having an oral teaching that addressed how the law of the Torah could be best used and applied as humanity developed.

BELOW Jesus' knowledge of the Jewish faith and its divine source enabled him to stand up to the Pharisees, one of the religious sects of his time. The Pharisees constantly challenged his knowledge and healing powers, but in vain.

THE PHARISEES' ORAL TRADITION

This oral tradition was their own interpretation of Kabbalah. Great Pharisaic rabbis such as Hillel and Gamaliel are both known to have been mystics in the Merkabah/Kabbalah tradition. The oral tradition was written down and turned into the Talmud in the 1st century CE, after the Jewish revolt against Rome that led to the destruction of the holy Temple in CE 70 and the exile of the Jewish people from their homeland. This was at about the same time as the Gospels were collated.

Once an oral teaching is written down it becomes crystallized and a new one develops. Kabbalah has moved on and grown since the writing of the Talmud and its sister commentaries, the Haggadah and Midrash. Many theological scholars believe in one source for the three Synoptic Gospels of Matthew, Mark and Luke. This has been referred to as a lost manuscript known as "Q". However, many modern scholars now believe that "Q" may not exist and that the Gospels were based on a mystical oral tradition instead, probably a Kabbalistic mixture of the Pharisaic and Essenic teachings of the time.

FOUR GOSPELS: FOUR WORLDS

Each of the Gospels of the New Testament represents one of the four Kabbalistic worlds. Matthew represents Asiyyah, the physical world, focusing on Jesus' physical kingship, his healing of people suffering from sickness and pain and on his tribal lineage through Joseph. Mark represents Yezirah, the psychological world, focusing on the development of Jesus as a healer and servant of humanity. The miracles of healing in this Gospel emphasize the exorcism of inner demons and the workings of the soul. Luke represents Beriah, the spiritual world, moving away from the tribal world of heritage and men. It is the gospel of the women, including the stories of Mary and Elisabeth and the well-known Nativity in the stable. In Luke the focus is on the spiritual family rather than the physical family. John represents Azilut, the divine world.

The other three Gospels are known as "synoptic", meaning that they all work together as a whole, but the Gospel of John is completely different. It tells the story of Jesus, the divine man, and has no physical details of his birth – as these are not relevant. Modern-day Christian Kabbalists teach that John is intended to be read as a personal meditation on spiritual development, with the reader in the place of the Christ.

ABOVE A 14th-century painting of Christ on the Tree of Life. Kabbalistically, the crucifixion is seen as Jesus showing the way across the "black hole" of Da'at to enter the spiritual world. The two thieves crucified with him in the Gospel of Luke hang from crosses at a lower level on the Tree of Life.

LEFT John the Baptist preaching in the wilderness. John's mission was to make the "paths" of the Lord "straight" (Matthew 3:1), seen as a reference to The Tree of Life, as Jesus was to remind the world of its direct link to the divine.

NEW TESTAMENT CLUES TO REINCARNATION

The principles of reincarnation were hotly debated within both the Jewish and Christian faiths nearly 2,000 years ago, with believers including St Gregory of Nyssa and the later discredited Church Father Origen, who taught of the pre-existence of souls. Even in the New Testament, references suggest reincarnation, the first being when Jesus asks his disciples who people believe he is, and they reply: "Some say that thou art John the Baptist: some, Elias; and others, Jeremias, or one of the prophets" (Matthew 16:14). In the Gospel of John the implication is clearer: "And his disciples asked him, saying, Master, who did sin, this man, or his parents, that he was born blind?" (John 9:2).

PART THREE

KABBALAH IN THE MIDDLE AGES

As Kabbalah is an oral tradition it could easily turn into "Chinese whispers" unless held firmly to the divine principles of its underlying structure. The original designs of the menorah and the Tabernacle, together with the mystical meanings of the letters of the Hebrew alphabet, were all-important until the 12th century, though written texts did start to appear from the 2nd century onward.

In the Middle Ages, an important Kabbalistic School of the Soul in Gerona updated the system into what is now known as the Tree of Life and Jacob's Ladder. This school's influence spread in France and Spain, with Kabbalah being studied by other religions, including Christianity and Islam. With the development of Lurianic Kabbalah in the 16th century, a new impulse was felt and the tradition became more complex as it moved in a different direction.

RIGHT A scholar travelling from one world to the next. Only the true spiritual seeker understands that beyond this physical world lies the invisible realm of cosmic law. This realization is based on direct experience and cannot be fully understood second-hand. This is why Kabbalah focuses on the different levels of creation – and the levels within the human being – to help the seeker transform his or her self through a series of personal revelations.

THE GREAT BOOKS

IN THE MIDDLE AGES, LEADING KABBALISTS TRIED TO RECORD THE TEACHINGS OF KABBALAH, INSPIRED BY THE INVENTION OF THE PRINTING PRESS. FOR THE FIRST TIME, MYSTICAL KNOWLEDGE COULD BE DISSEMINATED THROUGHOUT THE WORLD IN WRITTEN FORM. SEVERAL BOOKS ARE REFERRED TO AS SEMINAL BY ALL THE DIFFERENT KABBALISTIC GROUPS IN THE WORLD. THE ZOHAR, THE BEST-KNOWN KABBALISTIC TEXT, IS A TREATISE BASED ON A DISCUSSION AMONG LEARNED RABBIS WHO ARE TELLING STORIES AND OFFERING OPINIONS IN ORDER TO INTERPRET THE TEACHINGS. IT IS SIMILAR TO, BUT HAS A FAR DEEPER MYSTICAL CONTENT THAN, THE TALMUD, THE TRADITIONAL JEWISH COMMENTARY ON THE TORAH. OTHER IMPORTANT TEXTS INCLUDED SEFER YEZIRAH AND TOMER DEVORAH.

RIGHT The first page of the Sefer Yezirah (Book of Formation) showing the creation of the earth, the planets and the stars. Sefer Yezirah is often mistranslated as "the Book of Creation", but that would be Sefer Beriah. Yezirah is the world of the human psyche and soul.

BELOW A 19th-century engraving showing the display of the Torah to the congregation prior to the reading. The scroll has just been carried from the Ark, and the Torah mantle has been removed (it can be seen discarded on the left of the reading desk).

THE ZOHAR

The Zohar (Book of Splendour) is a group of five volumes written in a combination of medieval Aramaic and Hebrew. Three volumes are called Sefer ha-Zohar al ha-Torah, one Tikkunei ha-Zohar and the fifth, a collection of sayings and texts, Zohar Chadash. The first four books are mystical interpretations of the Torah, including discussions about the Holy One, how the universe is designed, the nature and origin of the human soul, good and evil, and the doctrine of immortality. The Zohar is highly symbolic and deeply obscure.

Dating the Zohar is a difficult challenge. It was first published in the 13th century by a Jewish writer in Spain. Moses de Leon claimed to have collated a number of ancient texts that he had discovered in a cave in Israel. Authorship of the book is attributed to Simeon ben Yohai, a rabbi who lived in the 2nd century CE. According to legend, Yohai and his son Elazar hid in a cave for more than a decade, during a time of persecution by Rome. Critics of the theory that the Zohar dates back so far point out that it refers to historical events of later times, but supporters regard these as Nostradamus-like predictions. Despite discord over its authenticity, within 50 years of its appearance in Spain, the Zohar became acknowledged and accepted by much of the Jewish community.

THE SEFER YEZIRAH

The Sefer Yezirah (Book of Formation) is less than 2,000 words long. It was known to be in existence in the 10th century CE but is thought to date back approximately 2,000 years. Sefer Yezirah contains mystical information about numbers and the letters of the Hebrew alphabet that are used for numerological interpretation of the Bible and other holy texts. Authorship is variously attributed to the Patriarch Abraham and to Rabbi Akiva, a 1st-century scholar and martyr. The book describes the universe as being divided into 10 Sefirot, 3 "mother letters", 7 "double letters" and 12 "elemental letters" corresponding to the Zodiac and the planets.

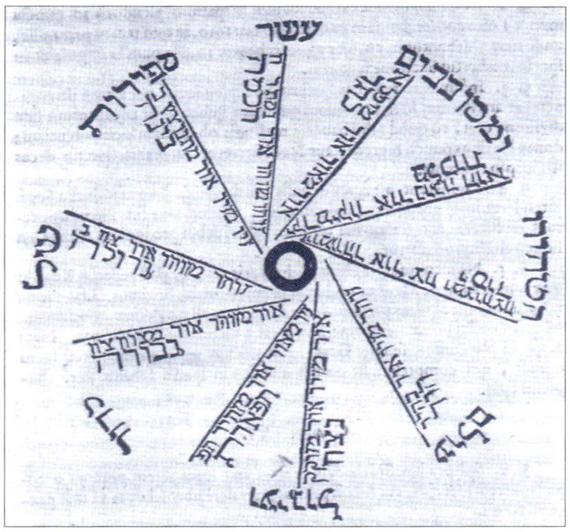

LEFT A 20th-century Israeli painting showing a rabbi with the Torah. The Torah is infinitely precious to the Jewish faith, being considered the direct word of God. Orthodox Jews attempt to obey all 613 laws as laid down in the books of Deuteronomy, Leviticus and Numbers, of which 248 are positive laws, as in "thou shalt", and 365 are negative, as in "thou shalt not." However, since several of the laws include Temple ritual, it is no longer possible for them all to be kept.

FAR LEFT Possibly the oldest existing depiction of the ten Sefirot of the Tree of Life, from the Sefer Yezirah, thought to date back approximately 2,000 years. The Tree as we know it now appears to be static, but it is a force in perpetual motion, as this Hebrew wheel of life demonstrates.

It includes details of "32 paths", which either refer to the 22 characters of the Hebrew alphabet plus the 10 Sefirot of the Tree of Life, or to the 22 characters of the Hebrew alphabet plus the numbers 1 through 10 that in Judaism represent the first 10 letters of the Hebrew alphabet. Many revisions of the book have led to disputes and claims of errors, but in the late 20th century, an American physicist and rabbi, Aryeh Kaplan, published a translation of the book, which is the version most used by Kabbalists today.

TOMER DEVORAH

Written by Rabbi Moses Cordovero in Safed, Palestine in the 16th century, Tomer Devorah (Palm Tree of Deborah) is named after the prophetess Deborah, from the Book of Judges. It is a Kabbalistic ethical and inspirational treatise on how humans can live in perfect imitation of God. It describes how to live the ten Sefirot of the Tree of Life, each of which represents a divine attribute. The book was first published in Venice in 1588.

MOSES DE LEON

Rabbi Moses ben Shem Tov de Leon (1240–1305) lived in Muslim Spain. Other than his involvement with the Zohar, he wrote *Sefer ha-Rimmon*, a book about mystical reasons for ritual laws. Rabbi Joseph ben Todros, a leading Kabbalist and scholar at the court of Alfonso X, attested to the Zohar being genuine after de Leon's death, but an equally valid story tells of a rich man offering de Leon's wife a large sum of money for the original text from which he had copied the work. She replied that there was no such text but that her husband had written it himself, attributing it to the famous Simeon ben Yohai so that it would be a good source of income.

BELOW A miniature Torah scroll. These sacred scrolls are individually hand-inscribed by sages and are of immense financial value, as well as having deep spiritual importance to the Jewish faith. In ancient times they were written on papyrus. The Torah was never produced in book form in antiquity because. at the time, books were made of the skins of animals that had not been sacrificed to the one God.

The Golden Age of Spain

The time known as the Golden Age of Spain was a period approximately between the 8th and 11th centuries when Spain was under Arab rule. It was not always a time of peace between Jews, Christians and Muslims as is often believed, and towards its end more than 1,500 Jewish families were massacred in Granada as Moorish rule began to dissolve. However, it was certainly a time when Jewish persecution was at a minimum and scholarship thrived. The relationship between Arabs, Christians and Jews was peaceful for the majority of this time, with all three faiths sharing information and mystical knowledge. In those days, the lines between spirituality, medicine, science and philosophy were blurred, and scholars took a holistic view.

RIGHT Engraving of the Hall of the Abencerrages in the Alhambra, an ancient mosque, palace and fortress complex of the Moorish monarchs of Granada, in southern Spain. The Alhambra, which means "The Red Castle" in Arabic, was the residence of the Muslim kings of Granada and their court.

BELOW The conquest of Muslim Toledo in 1085 by Christian King Alfonso VI of Spain, 1040–1109.

The Moorish occupation of Spain began in the 8th century, when a Berber Muslim army commanded by Tariq ibn-Ziyad crossed the Straits of Gibraltar from northern Africa. Roderick, the last of the Visigoth kings of Spain, was defeated, and by 719 CE, the Moors (from the Greek adjective *Mavros*, meaning black) had conquered the whole country. At that time, Islam was barely 100 years old and a very open faith that welcomed and nurtured scientific knowledge together with the wisdom and philosophy of foreign cultures – particularly of ancient Greece and India.

JEWISH LIBERTY

When the Moors conquered the cities of Cordoba, Malaga, Granada, Seville and Toledo they removed the restrictions that, under Visigoth-Christian rule, had oppressed the Jews, giving them complete religious liberty and requiring them only to pay a tribute tax. With the reign of Abd-ar-Rahman III and his son Al-Hakam II – known as the Caliphate of Cordoba – at the beginning of the 10th century, the Jews prospered, devoting themselves to science, commerce and industry, including the trade of silk and slaves. Southern Spain became an asylum for oppressed Jews from other parts of Europe.

LEFT The ancient walled city of Toledo, Spain, is the inspiration for the Toledano Tradition of Kabbalah. Toledo was the centre of religious tolerance and the sharing of knowledge throughout much of the Middle Ages, with Christian, Jew and Muslim working together on a mystical level to promote the unification of faiths.

BELOW Under Moorish rule, knowledge expanded across the Iberian peninsula and Spain experienced an era of religious understanding that was not witnessed again for 500 years. The Spanish Inquisition put an end to all diversity of faith. This 19th-century engraving shows the Moors being expelled from Spain.

KABBALAH IN TOLEDO

In 1085, the city of Toledo was re-conquered by Christian crusaders under the tolerant Christian king Alfonso VI of Castile. During the next 150 years, much Jewish and Moorish knowledge was collated, and made available to the rest of Western Europe.

Even under Muslim rule, Jews had continued to thrive and actively studied Kabbalah, the work of Aristotle and Arabian alchemy. What became known as the School of Toledo produced some of the first translations into Latin of works from the Arab world, notably the works of Averroes – an Andalucian-Arabian philosopher – and of Solomon Ibn Gabirol. According to legend, this Kabbalistic school included Jews, Muslims and Christians working together to promote a spiritual peace. This school's work is being emulated in the world today in the current Toledano tradition of Kabbalah. Because of the continuing mystical and scholarly work in Toledo, even after the "Golden Age" had ended, the Spanish Jewish community remained the most important scholastic and mystical Jewish group in the world.

THE COMING OF THE INQUISITION

The marriage of King Ferdinand of Aragon and Queen Isabella of Castile in 1469 heralded a powerful united Christian Spain that was to insist that all faiths converted to Christianity. All the mystical knowledge that had thrived in the preceding years was banned. The Spanish Inquisition was set up in 1478 under the Inquisitor-General Tomas Torquemada to seek out those who said they had converted, but who still practised their original faith in secret. Up to 2,000 people died through torture or execution over the following 14 years. In 1492 all remaining Jews were expelled from Spain. The Spanish Inquisition continued until the end of the Napoleonic Wars in 1835, with nearly 1,000 further deaths.

IBN GABIROL AND PLOTINUS

FEW MEDIEVAL PHILOSOPHERS INTERWEAVED THE THREE GREAT FAITHS OF JUDAISM, CHRISTIANITY AND ISLAM AS SUCCESSFULLY AS SOLOMON IBN GABIROL (1020–1058). IBN GABIROL WAS A JEWISH MYSTIC BUT ALSO A FOLLOWER OF THE GREAT SUFI MUHAMMAD IBN MASARRA (883–931). HE WROTE MORE THAN 300 POEMS AND APPROXIMATELY 20 BOOKS, THE BEST KNOWN OF WHICH ARE *KETER MALKHUT* AND *FONS VITAE* (*FOUNTAIN OF LIFE*). IBN GABIROL'S WORK WAS FREQUENTLY REJECTED BY HIS CONTEMPORARIES BUT INCREASED IN POPULARITY AFTER HIS DEATH, PARTICULARLY IN MYSTICAL CHRISTIAN COMMUNITIES. HIS IDEAS BECAME SO ABSORBED INTO THE DEVELOPMENT OF KABBALAH AND MEDIEVAL CHRISTIAN THOUGHT THAT GUILLAUME D'AUVERGNE, THE 13TH-CENTURY BISHOP OF PARIS, DECLARED THAT THE AUTHOR OF *FONS VITAE* WAS "THE MOST EXALTED OF ALL PHILOSOPHERS".

ABOVE This 1970 statue of Solomon Ibn Gabirol stands in the Jardines de la Alcazabilla, near to the Moorish fortress in the Spanish city of Malaga.

RIGHT The confessional prayer, part of Ibn Gabirol's Kabbalistic poem *Keter Malkhut*, is a vital part of the liturgy for Yom Kippur, the Jewish Day of Atonement, in which God is petitioned to include the names of the faithful in the Book of Life for the following year.

Ibn Gabirol studied philosophy through the Arabic translations available in Spain at that time, as well as Neoplatonism, including the work of the Jewish Neoplatonist Isaac Israeli from North Africa. Neoplatonic principles assisted Ibn Gabirol in helping Kabbalah to make the transition from experiential Merkabah mysticism to a mixture of mystical vision and philosophy. He wrote that neither vision nor intellect alone are enough to understand the universe.

IBN GABIROL'S WORK

By the age of 16, Ibn Gabirol had written a poem featuring all 613 Biblical commandments in a style known as "Azharot" and earned patronage from a high-ranking Jewish official at the regional Muslim court. However, he was frequently a provocative and immodest man and repeatedly fell out with his patrons and supporters, including the local Jewish community, who even denounced him as a heretic to the Islamic authorities.

The focus of Gabirol's work was the origin of the soul and its relationship with its divine source and with all other levels of existence, especially the physical world. He described the soul as being called into existence by the will of God, and wrote that it consists of three levels: the rational soul; the animate soul; and the vegetative soul. He also states that the soul is a cosmic principle and is not simply confined to existing in incarnated man.

Only three of his books survive: *Islah al-akhlaq*, (The Improvement of the Moral Qualities), a book on the ethics of correct behaviour; *Fons Vitae,* which outlines the universality of matter, the purpose of humanity and the communion of the soul with its source; and *Mibhar ha-Peninim* (Choice of Pearls), a collection of sayings and teachings. Much of Ibn Gabriol's religious poetry has been incorporated into the Judaic liturgy. Confusion remains over whether he died in 1058 CE aged 37, or in 1070 CE aged 48, and his death is surrounded by many stories, including one that he was murdered by a jealous rival. He left no record of a wife or family, which was extremely unusual for the period.

LEFT A gathering of the greatest philosophers, mathematicians and scientists of classical antiquity. Raphael's painting of *The School of Athens* shows Plato and Aristotle, the Greek philosophers that were considered most important, standing in the centre at the top of the steps. Their gestures correspond to their interests in the philosophical field. Plato is pointing upward towards Heaven, and Aristotle is gesturing toward the earth.

PLOTINUS AND KABBALAH

Neoplatonism is a philosophical system developed in Alexandria in the 3rd century CE by the philosopher Plotinus and his successors. It is an extension of the teachings of Plato mixed with mystical Judaic and Christian beliefs, and it focuses on the uniting of a human's soul with its own concept of God.

Neoplatonism was also deeply influenced by the work of the 1st-century Jewish philosopher Philo of Alexandria, who developed the concept of divinity known as the "Logos". This "Logos" is also what is referred to at the start of the Gospel of John – "In the beginning was the Word" (*logos* is Greek for "word").

In the 3rd century there were many Jews living in Alexandria, and the Jewish scriptures were being translated from Hebrew into Greek for the first time. As Alexandria is known to have been a centre for Jewish Kabbalists, it is certain that Kabbalah influenced the development of Neoplatonism, and the intellectuals of each culture learned much from each other with this synthesis of language and knowledge. Plotinus taught that the cosmos is the self-expression of the soul; the result of the soul's experience of its own mind (known as *nous*). The descent of the soul into physical reality is a necessary part of the unfolding of the divine intellect, or God. The rational soul naturally chooses good over evil but, if it forgets its source, it may produce evil actions (the modern Kabbalistic version of this would be the misuse of free will).

Plotinus' major successors – Porphyry, Iamblichus and Proclus – each developed aspects of Plotinus' thought, all of which reflected the Kabbalistic view of the purpose of creation being for God to behold God. Porphyry believed that knowledge of the planets and their relation to humankind was an important tool in self-knowledge. He also taught that the soul receives power from each of the planets – and that understanding them would help it on its path to righteousness. This is still the foundation of modern astrology today.

KETER MALKHUT

Ibn Gabirol's best-known work is *Keter Malkhut* (The Kingly Crown or The Crown of the Kingdom), a three-part Kabbalistic-philosophical treatise in poetical form, and companion to the *Fons Vitae*. *Keter Malkhut* is perhaps the greatest religious Hebrew poem of the Middle Ages, celebrating God and the wonders of creation.

The confession section of the poem is used on the Jewish festival of the Day of Atonement.

BELOW The 12th-century Islamic philosopher Ibn Rushd, known as Averroes, shown in an imagined conversation with 3rd-century Neo-platonist Porphyry. Both men worked with the teachings of Aristotle on the principle that there is no conflict between religion and philosophy.

Isaac the Blind

Very few biographical details exist about the life of the "father of Kabbalah", Isaac the Blind. Rabbi Yitzhak Saggi Nehor (1160–1235) is known to have lived in the French border town of Posquières for some time. It is not known for certain whether or not he was truly blind and, if so, for how much of his life. However, his influence led to the founding of the Kabbalistic School of Gerona in northern Spain, which was as important as the Toledo School. According to Kabbalistic tradition from the 13th century, Rabbi Isaac's eyes "never saw anything during his lifetime" (Me'irat Einayim, Munich Ms 17), yet several of his own writings contain complex details and discussions about the mystical importance of light and colour.

During his lifetime, Rabbi Isaac was given the Aramaic epithet "Saggi Nehor", meaning "of much light", in the sense of having excellent eyesight. Scholars believe that this could either have been an ironic epithet referring to his being physically blind or a reference to his being able to see at higher levels. He certainly wrote (or dictated) pamphlets during his lifetime, and much of his work was written down either by himself or by his followers. Some historians believe that Isaac the Blind wrote the Sefer ha-Bahir (Book of Brightness), an important Kabbalistic text named after Job 37:21 – "And now men see not the bright light which is in the clouds", but this is disputed.

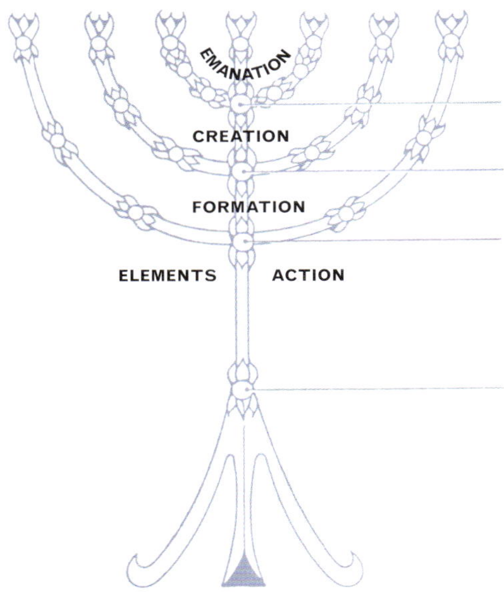

RIGHT Although the menorah had been used to interpret the teachings of the Tree of Life for centuries, advances in philosophy and the understanding of the mind necessitated an expansion of the principles within the structure. The updated design, accredited to Isaac the Blind, was also later to show a link with the Hindu chakra system.

RIGHT Dharmachakra, the wheel of life being turned by Yama, the Hindu Lord of Death. The wheel has 12 links depicting the 12 archetypes of humanity as demonstrated by the 12 signs of the zodiac and the 12 tribes of Israel.

The "Father of Kabbalah"

It was Isaac the Blind who named the ten Sefirot, and who placed a deeper – and lasting – emphasis on Platonic and Neoplatonic thinking by adopting the idea of metempsychosis, or the transmigration of souls. This is not the Buddhist or Hindu view that a human may reincarnate as an animal, according to how he or she has behaved in a previous life; rather, that we all have knowledge of the universe from our past experiences in different human bodies, and that our actions in one life influence the kind of life to which we will return.

Isaac the Blind's influence inspired the Kabbalists of Gerona in northern Spain, who subsequently developed the tradition into a more specific, grounded and practical system that could be learned and understood by many. This is why Isaac the Blind is considered the founder of Kabbalistic teaching as it has been passed down to us today. The 13th-century scholar and rabbi Bahya ben Asher named him "Father of the Cabala" in his commentary on the Pentateuch, section Wayishlah. Nobody knows for sure whether Isaac the Blind developed the designs of the Tree of Life and Jacob's Ladder that we know today, but he and his students were by far the most likely candidates. If so, their contribution to Kabbalistic understanding is of great significance.

THE SEFIROT

By Isaac the Blind's time, the idea of the Sefirot had developed from being the ten words or sayings with which the world was created into being specific vessels with differing characteristics, capable of receiving and then passing on the light of creation. Isaac the Blind named six of the Sefirot after the praises of God enumerated in the Book of Chronicles 29:11: "Thine, O Lord, is the greatness (Gedullah), and the power (Gevurah), and the glory, and the victory (Nezach), and the majesty (Hod) ... thine is the Kingdom (Malkhut)". The King James Bible mistranslates Tiferet as 'glory' rather than 'beauty', but the Hebrew is correct. The names of the Sefirot were amended in later years, but it was the naming of the attributes that made them definable – and led to the Tree of Life as we know it being developed and studied.

It was Rabbi Isaac's belief that contemplation of the aspects of each of the Sefirot, together with sacred intention (known as *kavanah*) would bring one into direct contact with the divine. This is best explained by the idea that the act of thinking of the attributes of the Sefirot (the world of Yezirah) would lift the consciousness to the realm of pure thought (the world of Beriah) and from there to the divine world of Azilut. As both Beriah and Azilut are devoid of form, it is impossible to contemplate them directly, other than as concepts. However, to think of their lower parallels in Yezirah would assist in raising the consciousness. All the Sefirot are linked to each other, so the energy of the matching Sefira in a higher world can be drawn down to a lower one.

ABOVE Gerona in Catalonia, northern Spain, overlooking the river Onyar, was the base for one of the most important schools of Kabbalah in the Middle Ages. When the Jews were expelled from Spain in 1492, their homes were blocked off and left empty. But in the early 1980s, the city began reclaiming its Jewish heritage through a project named "Bonastruc ca Porta". The project rediscovered and renovated the old Jewish quarter, and built a Kabbalah study centre and museum of Catalan Jewish history.

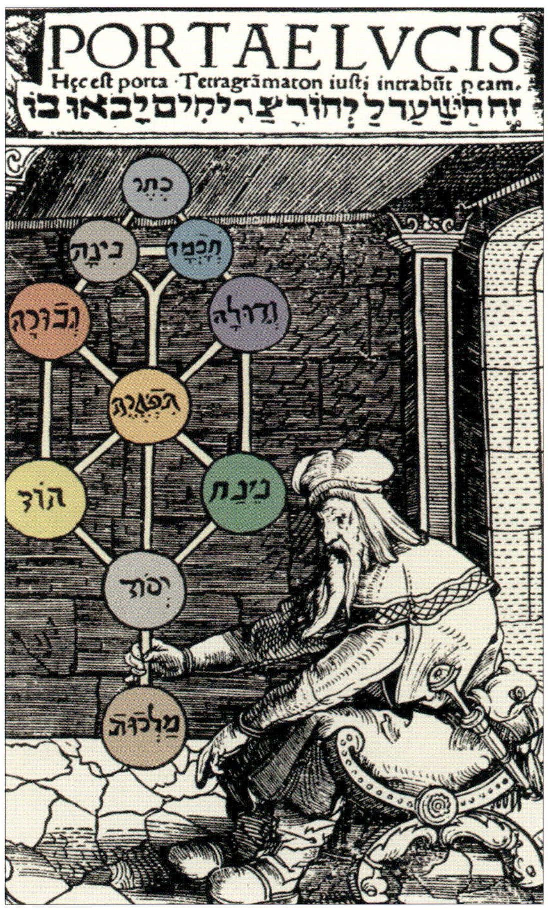

LEFT A Kabbalist contemplates the "tree" of the ten Sefirot on the Kabbalistic Tree of Life. This is one of the first printed illustrations of the Sefirot in this form, dating back to the mid-16th century. It appeared on the title page of Ricius' *Portae Lucis* –a Latin translation of a Kabbalistic work. The picture also shows two pillars, representing the columns of action and form, on the Tree of Life.

NACHMANIDES

NACHMANIDES, ALSO KNOWN AS RAMBAN (AN ACRONYM OF HIS NAME, RABBI MOSES BEN NACHMAN, OR MOSHE BEN NAHMAN), WAS BORN IN GERONA, SPAIN IN 1195. HE MADE HIS LIVING AS A DOCTOR BUT WAS BEST KNOWN FOR HIS COMMENTARIES ON THE HEBREW BIBLE, THE TALMUD, AND PHILOSOPHY. THE INFLUENCE OF THE GERONA SCHOOL OF KABBALAH IMBUED HIS WORK. HIS BIBLICAL COMMENTARIES WERE THE FIRST ONES TO INCORPORATE "KABBALISTIC" TEACHING. IN NACHMANIDES' LIFETIME, SPAIN HAD BECOME MOSTLY CHRISTIAN AND, ALTHOUGH THIS WAS BEFORE THE SPANISH INQUISITION, ANTI-JEWISH SENTIMENT WAS INCREASING. A POPULAR PRACTICE WAS TO HOLD A RELIGIOUS DEBATE BETWEEN A RABBI AND A PRIEST. IF THE RABBI LOST THE DEBATE, JEWS IN HIS AREA WOULD BE FORCED TO CONVERT TO CHRISTIANITY, BUT IF THE RABBI WON, NO ONE CONVERTED TO JUDAISM.

In 1263, King James of Spain called for a debate between Nachmanides and a Jewish convert to Christianity called Pablo Christiani. The topic was to be: Who was the Messiah and had he already come? Christians believed that Jesus Christ was the one Messiah, but Jews believed that the Messiah was still to come. Nachmanides, then 72 years old, won the debate, but the Church reacted immediately, ordering that he be tried on a charge of blasphemy. Conviction would have meant death, and so the philosopher was forced to leave the country in haste. He fled to Jerusalem, which was then in ruins after the Crusades, and helped to rebuild the shattered Jewish community; spiritually through his inspirational teaching and physically by building a synagogue.

RIGHT Orthodox Jewish men in the Ramban synagogue in Jerusalem. Nachmanides and his followers constructed the synagogue from a ruined house located on Mount Zion in just three weeks. He then set up a school that attracted hundreds of students, who journeyed to Jerusalem to be near the revered scholar, teacher, and leader. Both Sephardi and Ashkenazi Jews prayed and studied together in the synagogue for the next 300 years.

RIGHT A sculpture of Moses ben Maimon, known as Maimonides, located in the Jewish Quarter in Cordoba, Spain. This great Jewish scholar, philosopher and physician was forced to flee with his family to Fez, in Morocco, at the age of 23 to escape religious persecution at the hands of the fanatical Almohads in al-Andalus.

RETURN TO BASICS

Kabbalah and other forms of mysticism can be very complicated and obscure, but the honing of the tradition by Isaac the Blind and his followers enabled Nachmanides to further clarify the teachings. Instead of arguing over how many names there were for God, he wrote, simply: "The entire Torah are names of God". Nachmanides wrote widely on medical, philosophical and spiritual subjects. His last work was a commentary on the Torah that intended to give simple explanations and gentle interpretations. He tried to make *all* Jewish teachings more understandable by explaining the

nature of miracles, the idea the Creation came from nothing (Ayin Sof = the Absolute All), the omniscience of God, and Divine Providence.

Nachmanides taught that God is completely just, which means that there must be reward and punishment (karma). He was also believed to have written "Iggeret ha-Kodesh", a pastoral letter on marriage, holiness, and sexual relations. This criticizes the earlier Jewish teacher and philosopher, Maimonides, for saying that man's sexual nature was bad. Nachmanides wrote that as the body with all its functions is the work of God, everything to do with it is holy, as are normal sexual impulses and actions.

Nachmanides believed that it is acceptable for humans to ask angels to intercede for them with God (this was refuted by other rabbis who believed that only direct intercession was allowed). The view of Nachmanides is still reflected today in "Machnisay Rachamim", a request to the angels to intercede with God, which is part of the Jewish tradition of Selichot, said in the days before great festivals and fasts.

RIVALRY WITH MAIMONIDES

Rabbi Moses ben Maimon (1135–1204), better known as Maimonides, is one of the most respected of Jewish philosophers. He was a doctor but not a Kabbalist. Maimonides was born in Spain but lived most of his life in Egypt. His most influential work was *Moreh Nevuchim* (Guide for the Perplexed), which attempted to resolve apparent contradictions between the teachings of philosophy and the teachings of the Bible. Maimonides also wrote the 13 articles of faith, a reworking of which still appears in Jewish prayer books.

In Nachmanides' time, Maimonides's work was highly controversial and, although Nachmanides disagreed with the rationalisation of the Torah put forward by his fellow philosopher, and his rejection of miracles, he believed that these views were still worthy of respect. It was an indication of his gentleness of character that he worked tirelessly, although without success, to try and conciliate the two different schools of Judaism that were threatening to come to blows over whether Maimonides was right or wrong, possibly leading to his work being condemned as heretical.

LEFT A group of Kabbalists on the Mount of Olives outside Jerusalem. The city still exerts the same pull on followers of the world's three major religions as it did in Nachmanides' day. Nachmanides attracted hundreds of students to his school in Jerusalem after he and his followers built a synagogue from the ruins of a building on Mount Zion. His wish was to promote peace.

OTHER GREAT MEDIEVAL KABBALISTS

The term "medieval Kabbalists" is often used as a generality when referring to Jews who studied the system of numerology known as *gematria* – the giving of numbers to each of the 22 letters of the Hebrew alphabet and using them to look for patterns in the Torah for mystical insights. Identifiable medieval Kabbalists thrived in France and Spain in the 12th and 13th centuries. Rabbi Ezra ben Solomon of Gerona's commentary on the *Biblical Song of Songs* is one of the most important texts of the time, and *Treatise on the Left Emanation*, by Castilian Rabbi Isaac ha-Kohain, is a major work about the left-hand pillar of the Tree of Life, including the angelic principles of destruction.

LEFT An illuminated page from the Hebrew text *Moreh Nevuchim* (Guide for the Perplexed) by Moses Maimonides. The text says 'Part Two is complete and I will bring the next one with the help of the Lord.' In his day, Maimonides was considered as heretical for his strict interpretation of Jewish law. Today, however, his work is revered.

Moses Cordovero

WITH THE COMING OF THE SPANISH INQUISITION IN 1478 AND THE EXPULSION OF THE JEWS FROM SPAIN IN 1492, THE JEWISH NATION DISSIPATED THROUGHOUT EUROPE AND ISRAEL. SUCH A TRAGEDY AFFECTED ALL JEWISH THOUGHT AND, AS SCHOLARS AND SAGES SEARCHED FOR ANSWERS TO THE GREAT QUESTIONS OF LIFE, KABBALAH BEGAN TO OVERTAKE TALMUDIC SCHOLARSHIP IN JEWISH SPIRITUAL THOUGHT. BY THE 16TH CENTURY, THE ZOHAR HAD BEEN PRINTED IN ITALY AND BECAME AVAILABLE TO ALL – GREATLY INFLUENCING CHRISTIAN MYSTICS, AS WELL AS JEWS. MOSES BEN JACOB CORDOVERO, WHO WAS BORN IN 1522 AND DIED IN 1570 AT THE AGE OF 48, WAS ONE OF THE MOST RESPECTED TEACHERS OF THE ZOHAR AND A LEADING FIGURE IN A CIRCLE OF MYSTICS IN SAFED, ISRAEL.

RIGHT A Muslim woman being forcibly baptized into Christianity after the defeat of Granada by Ferdinand of Aragon in 1492. The Christian conquest and Inquisition forced Jews and Muslims to convert or leave. The exodus brought the finest Jewish mystics to Israel.

BELOW A Sephardi Jew in Safed, now a centre for Jewish art as well as a place of pilgrimage for Orthodox Jews and for students of Kabbalah. The three sit beside each other uncomfortably, especially when the non-orthodox pilgrims and artisans wish to view the synagogues where the sages learned and taught.

Cordovero's brother-in-law and teacher was Solomon ha-Levi Alkabetz, best known as the composer of "Lekhah Dodi", a Hebrew prayer that is still recited at sundown in synagogues each Friday night to welcome in the Sabbath before the evening services. Cordovero taught that the main difference between Kabbalah and philosophy was the solution to the problem of finding the essential link between God, the universe and humanity. He wrote that the Sefirot formed the bridge between the three, and emanated directly from God, suffusing life. This made God both transcendent (beyond knowing) and immanent (within everything). The understanding of the Sefirot, therefore, would reveal both God and self to any student.

As well as *Tomer Devorah* (The Palm Tree of Deborah), his written work included *Pardes Rimmonin* (The Garden of Pomegranates); *Or Ne'erav*, a much-needed introduction to the study of Kabbalah that made it more accessible to the layman; and *Ohr Yakar* (A Precious Light), a lengthy commentary on the entire Zohar. Cordovero was the first Kabbalist to be honoured by having the word 'the' added before his initials, and even today is known as the Ramak (an acronym taken from the first letters of his title and name – Rabbi Moses Cordovero).

THE LAST "ORIGINAL" KABBALIST

Cordovero's work was a further synthesis of the work of the 12th-century Kabbalists in Gerona and Toledo and a summary of the development of all the different trends in Kabbalah up to and including his own time. In 1550, he founded the school of Kabbalah in Safed. However, after Cordovero's death, Kabbalah was essentially rewritten by his successor, Isaac Luria, who began "the great heresy", a belief also held by the 1st-century Christian group known as the Gnostics (from the Greek word *gnosis* or knowledge), that when God created the universe, the Sefirot could not bear the power of the light and shattered. This was directly opposed to Cordovero's own work, which demonstrated that the Sefirot *could* contain the light and that God created the universe – and the world – perfect, as it says in the Book of Genesis. Luria's legacy lasted for the following 400 years, until the beginning of the Toledano tradition, which surfaced in the mid-20th century in England and has entirely returned to Cordovero's own mode of teaching.

SAFED IN ISRAEL

Safed (or Tzfat) is a hillside town in northern Israel that was a prominent centre of Kabbalistic teaching for many years after the expulsion of the Jews from Spain in 1492. It became home to both Moses Cordovero and Isaac Luria. According to legend, Safed was originally founded by one of Noah's sons after the great flood, though archaeology dates the town to the 2nd century CE. The area was revered even before becoming a centre of Kabbalistic teaching in its own right, as it is close to Meron, the burial place of Rabbi Simeon ben Yohai, alleged to be the author of the Zohar.

The Jewish population thrived here until the mid-18th century. However, their misfortunes returned when a series of plagues and earthquakes hit the town, virtually destroying the population in the years between 1742 and 1842. Safed was re-populated by immigrant Jews in the late 19th century. Most of its antiquities were destroyed by the earthquakes, but it is now a centre for artists, as well as being a re-established centre for Jewish learning and a place of pilgrimage for Kabbalists.

ABOVE The old cemetery of Safed. The Jewish tradition of placing a stone on a grave, instead of flowers, is said to originate from the fact that most graves were originally cairns, with visitors adding stones to show how many people had come to pay their respects.

LEFT The Jewish God had promised never to destroy his people again after the deluge, made famous by Noah's Ark in the Book of Genesis. For Jews facing the Inquisition in Spain and Portugal, it must have seemed as though that promise had been forgotten. In the Safed, the search for the reason why such things could happen brought forth a new generation of Jewish thinkers and mystical development.

SEPHARDI JEWS

The Jews of Spanish and Portuguese origin who were expelled from the Iberian Peninsula became known as "Sephardi" Jews and have a slightly different liturgy and attitude, both to Kabbalah and conventional Judaism, than "Ashkenazi" Jews, who originate from eastern Europe. It would seem logical that they took their name from Safed but, in fact, Sephardi comes from the name of an unidentified town called Sephar'ad in the biblical Book of Obadiah.

ISAAC LURIA

ISAAC LURIA, KNOWN AS "THE ARI" (LION), IS SO REVERED TODAY THAT IT IS EVEN SAID THAT THE PROPHET ELIJAH APPEARED TO HIS FATHER AT HIS BIRTH AND CIRCUMCISION. IN HIS DAY HE WAS BELIEVED TO BE THE MESSIAH, AND HIS TEACHINGS TRANSFORMED KABBALAH FOR FOUR CENTURIES. LURIA WAS BORN IN JERUSALEM IN 1534 AND, ON THE DEATH OF HIS FATHER, MOVED TO EGYPT. HE DEVOTED HIS LIFE TO THE STUDY OF THE TORAH AND THE ZOHAR. IN HIS EARLY 20S, HE BECAME A RECLUSE, LIVING ON THE BANKS OF THE NILE, EATING LITTLE, SPEAKING ONLY HEBREW AND VISITING HIS WIFE AND FAMILY ONLY FOR THE SABBATH. ACCORDING TO THE LEGEND, THE PROPHET ELIJAH TOLD HIM THAT HE WOULD SOON DIE, AND THAT HE WAS TO GO TO SAFED. IN 1569, LURIA RETURNED TO ISRAEL AND JOINED THE SCHOOL OF MOSES CORDOVERO IN SAFED. AFTER CORDOVERO'S DEATH, HE SET UP HIS OWN SCHOOL.

RIGHT Satan falling from heaven. According to Luria's teachings, evil entered the universe when the vessels of the Tree of Life cracked under the pressure of the light being poured into them by God. Some modern Lurianic Kabbalists say that God intended this mistake to happen so that humanity could be tempted by the dark side.

Isaac Luria spent much of his life focusing on spirits and ancient sages and channelling information to his disciples. Each Sabbath, he wore a four-layered garment in white to signify the four letters of the Ineffable Name of God, in preparation for the coming of the Messiah, which he foretold to be imminent. Luria never proclaimed himself to be the Messiah, but many of his followers were convinced that he was the Anointed One. He was believed to be able to heal the sick, perform miracles and speak to animals. He died at the age of 38, the victim of an epidemic sickness.

RIGHT A late 16th-century Russian icon of the fiery ascent of the prophet Elijah to heaven. Elijah was said to be Isaac Luria's guide and to have inspired him to move from Egypt to Israel to set up his own school of Kabbbalah.

THE GREAT HERESY

The uniqueness of Luria's primary theory was that God made a mistake during the Creation, and that the purpose of humanity was to redeem that error. His teaching asserts that, as the Divine Light from Ayin Sof poured into universe, it was too great for the Sefirot to bear. The three highest Sefirot, being made from the purest substance because of their proximity to Ayin Sof, were able to bear the glory of the Divine Light, but the seven below them were farther away from the source and therefore of less purity. They were unable to contain the light and shattered. The Holy One then withdrew the focus of the light from them and transformed them into images known as *partzufim* (from the Hebrew word meaning "faces"). The lynchpin of Luria's teaching is that if God had at first created these images instead of the Sefirot, there would have been no evil in the world, and consequently no reward and punishment; for the source of all evil is the broken Sefirot, or vessels (Shevirat ha-Kelim), while the light of Ayin Sof creates only that which is good. Humanity's task is to assist in the Tikkun Olam, the "Restoration of the World".

EXTERNAL EVIL AND KARMA

This new version of the old teaching appealed to Luria's followers – Jewish people who had been sent into exile by the Inquisitions of Spain and Portugal. An impartial evil force that was created at the dawn of time being responsible for their pain and persecution was easier to understand than the idea that the innocent had suffered either because they themselves had been evil in a previous life or because they had ignored or not noticed signs and portents of catastrophe to come and been unwilling to leave their homes and venture into the unknown.

LURIA'S DIAGRAMS

Isaac Luria is believed to have worked out an increasingly complicated system of diagrams demonstrating his theories – although Luria himself wrote very little, and these were only revealed through the writings of his pupil and successor Hiyyim Vital. The extreme complexity of the images was too much for most Kabbalists to study. Luria preferred his own designs to the diagram of Jacob's Ladder and, as his work flourished, the older design became unfashionable and disappeared from popular knowledge. It was replaced by many different interpretations of how the four Trees of Life of different worlds fitted together, many of which contradicted each other. Jacob's Ladder returned to the public domain in the 1970s with the resurgence of pre-Lurianic Kabbalah through the Toledano tradition.

ABOVE Although the old graveyard at Safed is filled with the graves of great Kabbalistic scholars, it is Luria's grave that attracts by far the most pilgrims. The great sage died very young, at the age of 38, but his legacy has spread far and wide.

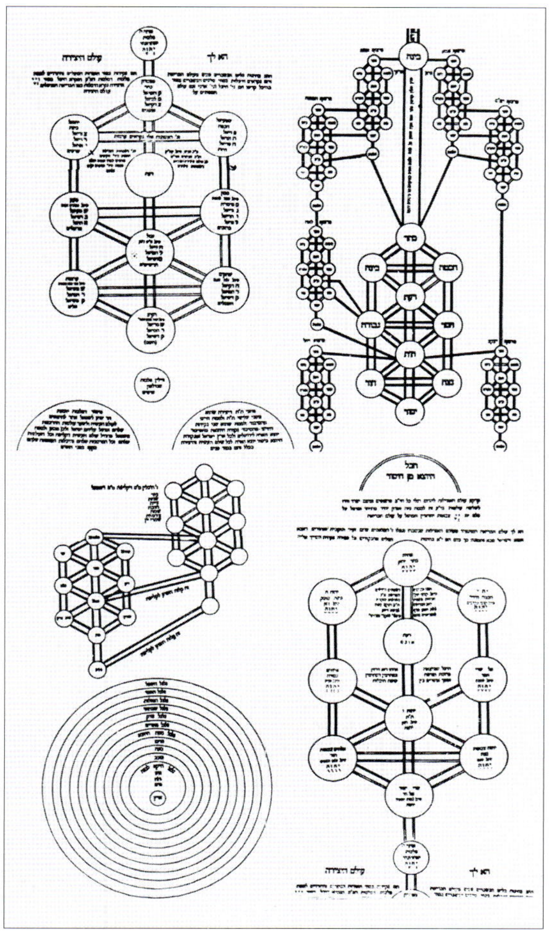

LEFT Isaac Luria's interpretation of the Tree of Life included the development of more complex diagrams than had been seen before. These demonstrated his theory of "God's mistake" during the Creation and were frequently too difficult for students to comprehend. It was at this time that the original Jacob's Ladder was forgotten – or, at least went underground for the following 400 years.

LURIA'S LEGACY

The Lurianic doctrines of shattered vessels and the work of restoration, translated as exile and redemption, took off like wildfire. Ironically, Luria himself only wished his teaching to be available to his own school of initiates, and his disciple, Hayyim Vital, attempted to control the teachings in vain. Luria himself became a Kabbalistic celebrity when *Shivhei ha Ari* (In Praise of the Ari) and *Toldot ha Ari* (The Life of the Ari) were published at the beginning of the 17th century. The stories in these two books are still used today to demonstrate the Messianic-like prowess and knowledge of the Ari.

THE SPREAD OF KNOWLEDGE

FROM THE 16TH CENTURY, ANYONE COULD BUY A COPY OF THE ZOHAR OR THE BOOKS BY THE KABBALISTS FROM SAFED, AND KABBALAH BECAME AVAILABLE TO ANY MYSTIC OR RELIGIOUS SEEKER. LURIA'S FAME BACKED BY CORDOVERO'S SYNTHESIS OF PREVIOUS KABBALISTIC TEACHINGS, INCLUDING HIS DIGEST OF THE ZOHAR, MEANT THAT THE TRADITION COULD BE UNDERSTOOD IN THE WIDER WORLD FOR THE VERY FIRST TIME. HOWEVER, AS THE KNOWLEDGE SPREAD, DIFFERENT VERSIONS BEGAN TO TAKE ROOT. THE LOSS OF JACOB'S LADDER, AND THE COMPLEXITY OF LURIA'S DIAGRAMS, TOGETHER WITH A LACK OF SCHOLARSHIP OF THE TORAH AND THE KABBALISTIC STORIES IN IT, LED TO DIVERSITY AND CONFUSION. WHILE MUCH GOOD WORK WAS STILL DONE BY MYSTICS SUCH AS ROBERT FLUDD, MISINFORMATION – SUCH AS THE IDEA THAT THE MESSIAH WAS DUE AT ANY TIME – WAS ALSO DISSEMINATED.

RIGHT *The Alchemist's Experiment Takes Fire*, a 17th-century painting by Dutch artist Hendrick Heerschop. Many students of alchemy focused on the idea of transforming physical substances, rather than understanding that inner transformation at all levels was the goal of the true alchemist.

The Reformation, which divided the Christian Church into Catholic and Protestant denominations, officially began in 1517, when German monk Martin Luther publicly opposed the Pope over the sale of indulgences – the giving of alms or services to the Church in return for partial forgiveness of sins by church officials.

KABBALAH AND THE REFORMATION

Martin Luther himself translated the Bible from Greek and Hebrew into German, and all the countries of Europe followed his example by translating the Scriptures into their own languages. The Hebrew Scriptures were translated into German in 1506 by the philosopher Johannes Reuchlin, in his lexicon *De Rudimentis Hebraicis.* The publication of the Zohar followed 50 years later in Italy.

With the establishment of the printing press, sacred texts could be printed and spread around the world. This freedom of information meant that many Christian mystics began to examine the Jewish tradition with interest. Reuchlin himself was a member of the Platonic Academy at Florence and wrote two books on Kabbalah: *De Verbo Mirifico* in 1494 and *De Arte Cabbalistica* in 1517. Both books were virtually incomprehensible to the layman, as they were devoted to *gematria* (a mathematical system that works on a correspondence between the ten Sephirot and the 22 letters of the Hebrew alphabet), and to mysterious names and figures.

RIGHT Sir Francis Bacon, Lord Verulam, and Viscount St Albans, philosopher and statesman at the courts of Queen Elizabeth I and James I of England. Sir Francis was a man of great intellect, but was not able to live up to the high ideals in which he believed. In 1621 a parliamentary committee on the administration of the law convicted him of corruption, and he left public life to focus on writing.

KABBALAH AND SCIENCE

The origins of the Royal Society, originally known as the Royal Society of London for the Improvement of Natural Knowledge, lie in an "invisible college" of natural philosophers who began meeting in the mid-1640s to discuss the ideas of Francis Bacon (1561–1626) and his book *The New Atlantis.* Sir Isaac Newton, Sir Christopher Wren and John Evelyn (Charles II's chosen architect to rebuild the city of London after the great fire of 1666) were all prominent members of the Society. Bacon, a member of Queen Elizabeth I's court, was a leader in the scientific revolution of the 17th century with his new "observation and experimentation" theory, which has influenced the way science has been conducted ever since. In his day, scientific study included the occult and alchemy. Bacon is believed to have studied Kabbalah, and his aphorism "knowledge is power" is well known. The German mathematician and philosopher Gottfried Wilhelm Leibniz (1646–1716), who invented the differential and integral calculus (independently of Sir Isaac Newton), is said by his biographers to have been profoundly influenced by Kabbalah.

KABBALAH AND FREEMASONRY

Freemasonry is a very old, secular, fraternal society that requires a belief in a supreme being. Its origins are obscure and, over the centuries, as various Grand Lodges emerged, its mystical beliefs were lost. However, there are distinct links to Kabbalah through the design of famous churches by great architects and stonemasons, dating back to the 12th century. The principle of the four worlds is demonstrated through the nave (Asiyyah, the physical world), the choir (Yezirah, the psyche), the sanctuary (Beriah, spirit) and the tabernacle (Azilut, divinity). In addition, the Masonic "rule of three" – in a church represented by a central aisle with two side aisles – is the equivalent of the three pillars of the Tree of Life.

Masonry as we know it today was first starting to form in the 16th century, at the time of the Renaissance, when writers such as Shakespeare, Milton, Dee, Bacon and Fludd were demonstrating knowledge of the Hermetic and Kabbalistic traditions. However, it is more likely that the 17th-century fears of witchcraft that were rife during the reign of the superstitious James I of England (originator of the King James Bible) led to the Masons becoming a secret society.

ABOVE The great gothic cathedral of Chartres is filled with astrological symbology, including an astrological clock, a stained-glass window depicting the signs of the zodiac, and the 12 zodiacal signs also carved on the north door and west front of the cathedral.

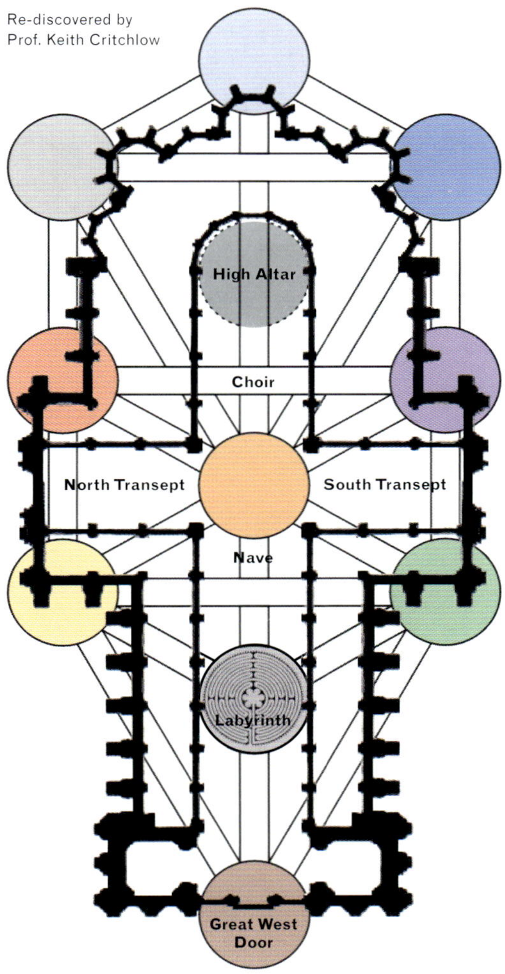

LEFT The internal design of Chartres Cathedral fits perfectly on to the Tree of Life, as do the designs of many other great European churches, including King's College Chapel, Cambridge, England. The rose window here is designed perfectly to represent Da'at. Should that part of the edifice fall, it would land directly on to the labyrinth (Yesod).

THE CATHEDRAL AT CHARTRES

Chartres Cathedral is thought to have been built with a synthesis of the Judaic, Islamic and Christian mystical knowledge of the times. Kabbalistic knowledge was certainly known and understood throughout the Masonic fraternity of medieval times, when 'mason' meant a builder of sacred edifices rather than a member of a secret fraternity. Chartres Cathedral was first begun in 1145, but then reconstructed over a 26-year period after a great fire in 1194. It is also a magnificent example of French Gothic art.

THE FALSE MESSIAH

THE TEACHINGS OF LURIANIC KABBALAH EMPHASIZED THE IMMINENT ARRIVAL OF THE MESSIAH, SO THOSE WHO STUDIED KABBALAH WERE AS EMOTIONALLY READY FOR THE FINAL REDEMPTION AS 1ST-CENTURY CHRISTIANS WHO EXPECTED THE END OF DAYS AND THE SECOND COMING OF CHRIST. IRONICALLY, MEDIEVAL CHRISTIAN LEADERS HAD INDEPENDENTLY PREDICTED THAT CHRIST WOULD COME IN 1666, AND THAT WAS THE EXACT TIME WHEN WORD SPREAD ACROSS JEWISH EUROPE THAT ALL HOPES HAD BEEN FULFILLED. THE JOY WAS SHORT-LIVED AND THE STORY OF THE "FALSE MESSIAH", SHABBETAI ZVI, DROVE KABBALAH UNDERGROUND – DERIDED AND CONSIDERED DANGEROUS AND FALSE. TO AVOID ANY FURTHER CATASTROPHES, RABBIS PROCLAIMED KABBALAH WAS ONLY SUITABLE FOR MEN OVER THE AGE OF 40 WHO HAD FAMILIES.

Shabbetai Zvi, a brilliant but mentally unstable scholar and mystic now known as the False Messiah, was born in Smyrna, Turkey, in 1626. He was a committed Kabbalist, and his religious ecstasies and revelations entranced some and outraged others. He became a celebrity of his time, travelling around the Middle East, but his behaviour was erratic and he was expelled from the town of Salonica for performing a wedding service with himself as the bridegroom and the Torah as the bride.

RIGHT The house of Shabbatai Zvi in Izmir (formerly Smryna), Turkey, has a commemorative shrine in the courtyard. Zvi was married three times while in Izmir, his first two marriages ending in divorce through non-consummation. His third wife, Yocheved Filosof claimed that after Zvi's death, her brother had inherited his soul.

RIGHT Shabbatai Zvi blessing some of his followers. It appears that Zvi truly believed that he was the Messiah. Such delusions are common among spiritual seekers who aim for comprehension of the higher worlds before they have their own psyches under discipline.

DELUSION AND DOWNFALL

His greatest delusion and ultimate downfall came after meeting a self-proclaimed prophet called Nathan of Gaza, in 1665, in Palestine. Nathan declared that Shabbetai Zvi was the long-awaited Messiah and would throw off the yoke of the Sultan of Palestine. Shabbetai Zvi believed him and, pronouncing the Ineffable Name of God (which was forbidden), he appointed himself 12 disciples and began riding around Palestine on horseback preaching to crowds, building a fervent

LEFT The Golden Gate (the south wall of the Temple) in Jerusalem. This is the gate through which Jews believe that the Messiah will come into the city at the "End of Days". It has been walled up and a graveyard set before it by Muslims, to prevent the Messiah from coming. Jewish law forbids a priest to cross a graveyard.

following and promising to overcome the Sultan and Islam. His fame spread to Europe, with Jews repenting and preaching in Messianic frenzy and supporters writing enthusiastic tracts in his praise. Thousands of Jews sold their homes to provide themselves with money to travel to the new Utopia of the Holy Land.

The Sultan could only allow such behaviour for so long and, within a year, he had Shabbetai Zvi placed under house arrest. When that did not stem the Messianic tide, the pretender was taken before the Sultan, who offered him the choice of death or conversion to Islam. Shabbetai Zvi chose conversion and put a turban on his head immediately. The Sultan gave him the title of "Keeper of the Palace Gates" and a pension of 150 piastres a day.

Some of his followers believed that whatever Shabbetai Zvi did was right and began studying Islam, but the vast majority of Jews were devastated. For the next two years, Shabbetai played a kind of double game between Islam and Judaism, telling the Sultan that he was working to bring Jews to convert to Islam. Many of his Kabbalistic followers did just that. However, the Sultan discovered that he was double-dealing and sent the False Messiah into exile, where he later died. After this disaster, the Jewish authorities clamped down firmly on the study of Kabbalah, deeming it too dangerous to be available to the masses.

RESTRICTIONS ON STUDENTS

After the debacle of the False Messiah, rabbis placed a stricture on Kabbalah that it should only be studied by men over 40 who had a family. This was to ensure that the student had proved himself as an orthodox Jew by following the Commandments and honouring Jewish tradition in raising a family. This was not entirely new: one of St Jerome's letters, dating back to the 4th century, mentions a Jewish tradition that the study of the beginning and end of the Book of Ezekiel (source of the Merkabah tradition) was forbidden before a man was 30.

LEFT Christ's triumphant entry into Jerusalem to the great joy of the Jewish people, from a 14th-century Armenian Gospel. The coming of the Messiah will mean the "End of Days". To Kabbalists, the final coming of the Messiah will be when all of humanity has reached a perfect level of being.

PART FOUR

PRACTICAL KABBALAH

Kabbalah can be astonishingly complex and, with several different traditions operating in the modern age, it can also be hard to know where to start studying how Kabbalah works. The purpose of Kabbalah is to understand the relationship between God, the universe and humanity. Kabbalah believes that the goal of humanity is to become perfect so that each of us can fulfil our part as a divine spark in the Divine Man, Adam Kadmon. Every human being's path to the divine is unique, and every person's interpretation of the two great Kabbalistic diagrams, the Tree of Life and Jacob's Ladder, is an individual quest. As well as the two main structures of Kabbalah, different traditions also study astrology, numerology and meditation on the names of God.

RIGHT *Jacob's Ladder,* by William Blake, shows the angels ascending and descending the levels between earth and heaven.

The Tree of Life

The Tree of Life is a diagram showing the principles first demonstrated in the design of the menorah in the biblical Book of Exodus. There are four Trees of Life in Kabbalistic teaching, but this one is the most studied. It represents the human psyche and soul, and is called Yezirah, the world of form. By "form" it means the individual make-up of a human, rather than the structure. The structure is two arms, two legs, one backbone and so on. The form is the colour of the skin and hair, and the build, the astrological blueprint and the karmic and hereditary factors that make each person an individual. The Tree has 10 principles or Sefirot (from SPHR, the Hebrew root for circle or sapphire), 3 pillars or columns, 22 paths and 16 triangles or triads, each representing an important aspect of each human being's psyche.

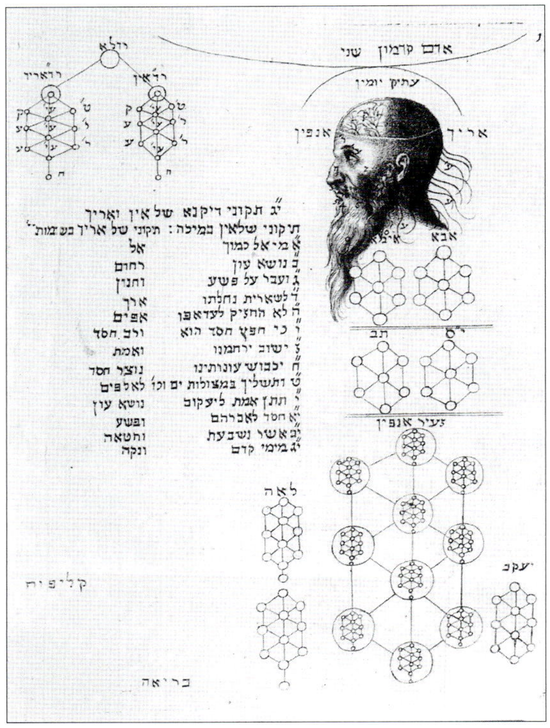

RIGHT In this 17th-century diagram by Knorr von Rosenroth, the Tree is shown as having either ten or seven Sefirot. Above the seven is the image of Adam Kadmon. The seven lower Sefirot represent everyday life, with the Supernal Triad of Binah–Keter–Hokhmah representing the divine parts of our selves. Many Kabbalistic exercises, including the "Counting of the Omer" – the experiencing of the levels of the days between the festivals Passover and Shavuot – only use the seven lower Sefirot.

The Tree is viewed either as though it were a person facing away from the viewer (the left-hand side of the Tree being the left-hand side of the body and the right-hand side, the body's right side) or as if it were being viewed in a mirror, which gives the same effect. In the Book of Exodus (33:20), the Lord says to Moses: "Thou canst not see my face: for there shall no man see me, and live." So, as the Tree of Life represents the image of God, the Jewish tradition is to view it from the back.

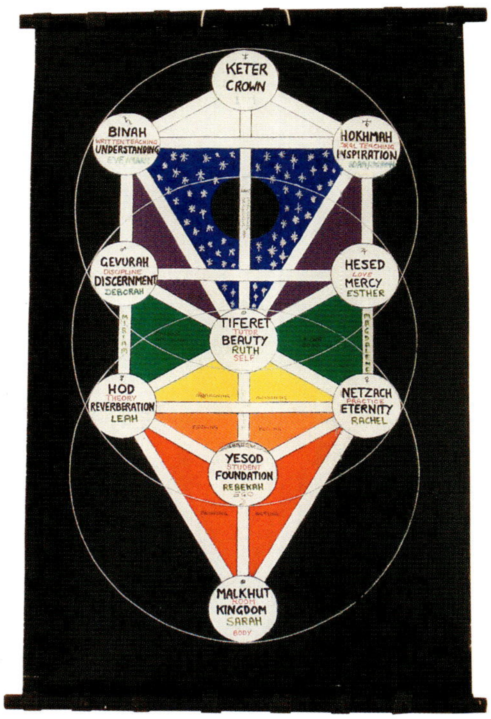

RIGHT One of the most valuable exercises the student of Kabbalah can do is to paint his or her own Tree of Life and Jacob's Ladder. Mistakes made in the process and the information placed on the diagram are comprehensive indications of a student's psychological development .

BASIC PRINCIPLES

The Tree of Life is the Kabbalistic world of Yezirah (the psychological level). It is a blueprint of a human being; like an astrological chart, it shows the inherent strengths and weaknesses of a person's psyche and soul. The left-hand pillar represents the passive or receptive aspects of the psyche, from thought processes through to the concepts of understanding and boundaries. The right-hand side

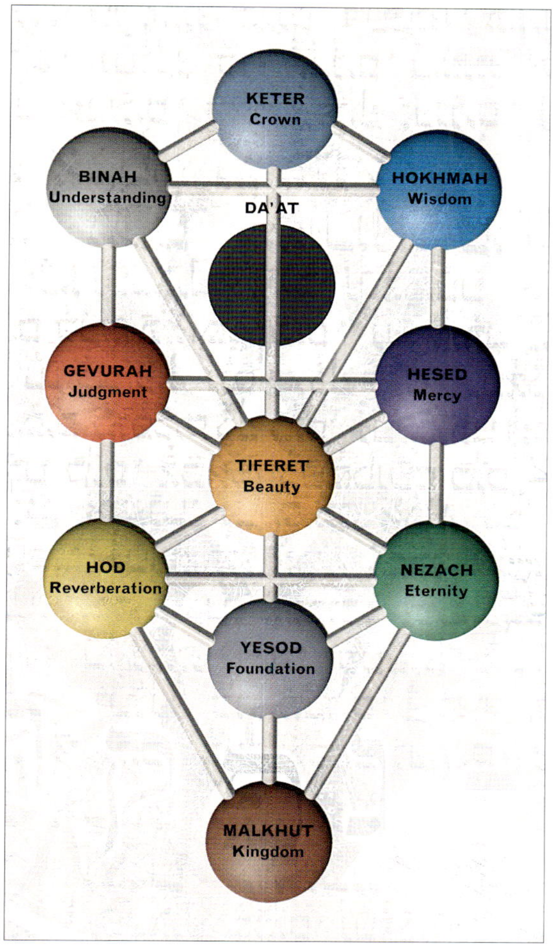

LEFT The ten Sefirot of the Tree of Life represent a part of each individual's psychological make-up. Many of us over-balance towards either the pillar of severity (left) or mercy (right), but we all experience the central column of physical body (Malkhut), ego (Yesod) and self (Tiferet), and we all have access through Da'at to the higher worlds.

represents the active or giving aspects, from sexuality to generosity and creativity. The central column represents a person's consciousness and the part of each human that has the power to use free will to rise above physical and psychological habits and limitations.

Each horizontal line represents a level of consciousness, or thinking, the lowest line being known as "the liminal line", below which we all operate through habit or social conditioning. The middle line represents the level of the human soul, and the top line represents access to the concept of the Higher Self or spiritual realm.

The Tree works at many different levels, and modern Kabbalists often colour it in a way similar to the Hindu chakra system, to show the levels of human consciousness. The red level corresponds to the base chakra – the principle of the life force; the orange to the gonadic chakra – ego and sexuality; the yellow to the solar plexus chakra – the self; the green to the heart chakra – love and fear; the blue to the throat chakra – communication and clairaudience; the purple to the third eye chakra – insight and clairvoyance; and the white to the crown chakra – the higher self.

THE TEN SEFIROT

The most commonly-used Hebrew names for the ten Sefirot are: Malkhut (Kingdom), Yesod (Foundation), Hod (Reverberation), Nezach (Eternity), Tiferet (Beauty), Gevurah (Judgement), Hesed (Mercy), Binah (Understanding), Hokhmah (Wisdom) and Keter (Crown). The spellings of the Hebrew words can vary; for example, Tiferet is also known as Tifareth and Hesed as Chesed.

More modern interpretations of the names of the Sefirot are: Malkhut (Bodily Impulses), Yesod (Ego and Social Conditioning), Hod (Thought and Intelligence), Nezach (Sexuality and Creativity), Tiferet (the Self; or Place of Truth), Gevurah (Discernment and Discipline), Hesed (Love and Expansion), Binah (Boundaries and Inner Insight), Hokhmah (Inspiration and Spiritual Drive) and Keter (the Higher Self, or Place of the Messiah). There is also what is known as the non-Sefira of Da'at – the black hole in the top centre of the Tree. This is a representation of the "leap of faith" required of human free will to let go of physical and psychological habits and limitations and access the spiritual worlds.

BELOW The designs of the Tree of Knowledge and Tree of Life have inspired artists for centuries. Here the original design of the Menorah can be seen through the arms of the humans reaching out for the apples – so merging both Trees into one.

DRAWING THE TREE

Making a freehand drawing of the Tree of Life is a way of identifying the psychological make-up of an individual person. Drawing fatter Sefirot on the right-hand side of the Tree will indicate a person who is very outgoing or perhaps over-generous. Fatter Sefirot on the left-hand side indicate a person who is more introspective, theoretically-minded and perhaps over-fearful or judgemental. Missing out a pathway will mean that there is a lack of communication between the relevant parts of the psyche. It is important to note that, like the human aura, the human "Tree" changes minute by minute, but general trends can be observed accurately.

Levels of the Tree

The Yeziratic Tree of Life has many levels, but the most useful to understand are the human, animal and vegetable ones. No level is necessarily more important than another. There is a tendency among practitioners of spiritual work to focus on the human and spiritual and to disregard work at a more mundane level. Kabbalah teaches that unless we have a strong foundation, no spiritual work can succeed. The vegetable levels are the three triads around Yesod, representing the human ego-consciousness. The animal level is represented in the triad between Hod, Nezach and Tiferet. This is the social and power-base part of the psyche, where humans jostle for position in the "tribe". The human level is represented by the soul triad, formed by Gevurah, Hesed and Tiferet, and it is where the human soul resides.

ABOVE Kabbalah teaches that heaven and hell are within the human psyche at all times, and that there will be no "Judgement Day", as depicted here. Rather, at death, we will assess our own level of development during life with our discarnate peers before deciding what path to take in the next life.

The Vegetable Level

The vegetable level is the part of our psyche that science now knows to be the "reticular system" of the brain. This is a filtering device that ensures that our brains do not get overloaded with new stimuli. The human ego is trained from the day of our birth to make decisions for us about what is relevant. It works entirely on automatic pilot and is trained by repetition. When someone learns to drive they begin the lessons at a conscious (human) level and have to focus very clearly on what is being done, co-ordinating actions to make the car work safely. However, once they have learned to drive, the majority of the requirements of driving are done without conscious thought; instead they are carried out by the ego. The reason why this level is called "vegetable" is because it is concerned with the psyche's everyday needs – seeking light, warmth, food and sex; being concerned with reproduction and then ageing and dying. Embracing spiritual growth is contrary to the normal drives of nature, and the vegetable level often resists development.

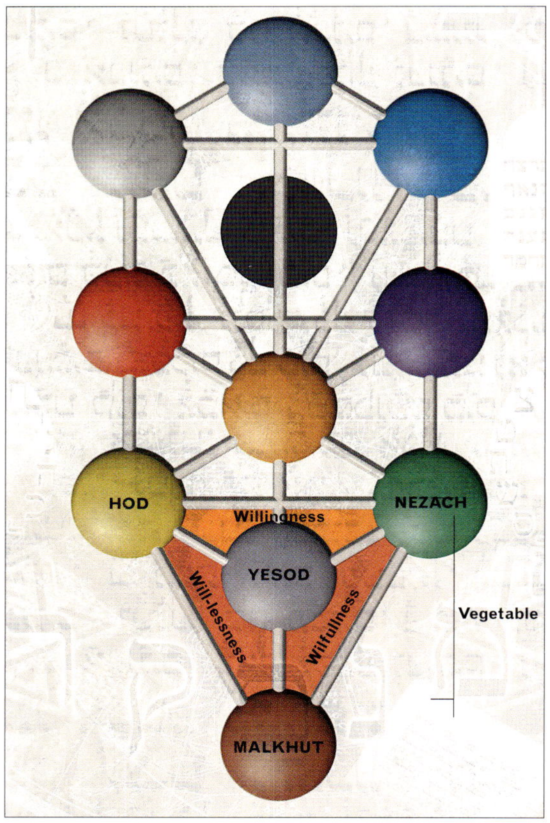

RIGHT The vegetable level of humanity is the part of us that does not want to take responsibility for our lives or change, preferring to blame others for perceived failings. We only become truly "human" when we do take full responsibility for our own life and level of happiness.

THE ANIMAL LEVEL

Politicians and business people and those who want to get to the top of their profession are animal people, but everyone has the ability to be an animal person. Even the most shy, modest and retiring person can become as brave as a lion and stand up to any opposition if the life of their child is threatened, for example. For some people, however, the animal level is the be-all and end-all of life. They must be the most powerful, the most famous or the most respected person in their field, and they may neglect their home, family and physical health.

Both the animal and vegetable levels are tribal, with people finding their place in the hierarchy and being subject to the karma both of their family and their country. All families develop their own hereditary karmic patterns, and countries also get back what they put out. Countries that colonize or invade other countries will, in turn, be colonized or invaded. A person living in such a country would experience its karma whether or not they had been involved in the actions that created it.

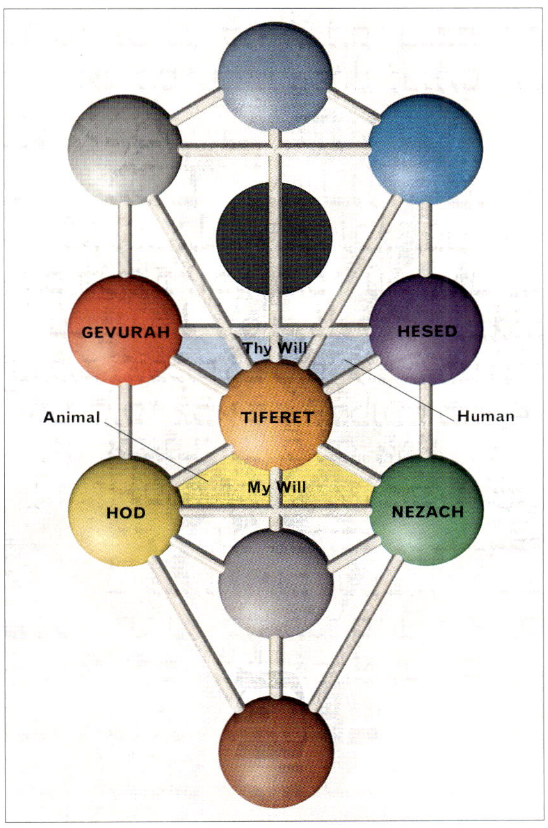

THE HUMAN LEVEL

At this level, we are able to access and use free will. Free will means making conscious decisions, rather than taking a well-trodden path or following social norms. People who work from the soul level have the ability to override the karma of family or country by observing trends and making decisions, either to become involved in or to move away from a certain situation. Being human often means being brave enough to leave everything familiar behind and start again.

ABOVE The Supernal Triad can be compared to the way that colour is created from light. The focused beam (Hokhmah) is emitted from the light source (Keter). The prism through which the light is scattered is Binah. None of these three contain colour on their own, yet together they produce a rainbow of seven colours, which represent the remaining seven Sefirot of the Tree of Life.

THE SPIRITUAL LEVEL

Humanity has access to the spiritual level of the four worlds from the Sefira of Tiferet, which is also the Malkhut of the spiritual world. The "Supernal Triad" of Binah, Hokhmah and Keter represent the spiritual level within a human's psyche, while acting as the Hod and Nezach of the spiritual world of Beriah. The Da'at of Yezirah overlays the Yesod of Beriah. It is this one Sefira, linking two worlds, that enables us to experience direct understanding of the spiritual realm. Da'at equates to the throat chakra that is the place of clairaudience – communication with spirit or with the archangelic realms.

LEFT The levels of human will are demonstrated by our physical development. A baby is will-less; it may want food or comfort, but it cannot identify needs. It then becomes wilful, as in the "terrible twos", then willing to learn like the interested school child. Between Hod, Tiferet and Nezach humans experience "my will", which is the development of self apart from the tribe. The soul triad is when we hand that developed will over to God.

GOOD AND EVIL

In Kabbalistic terms good and evil exist at the level of the soul, where conscious choice can be made between right and wrong. Plants and animals do not perform evil acts, and neither do humans at the vegetable or animal levels. This does not mean that people do not do things that hurt or wound – people are frequently upset, hurt or even killed by actions taken at those lower levels. However, these actions are instinctive or intended for self-protection rather than from a cool, considered, conscious wish to hurt or destroy.

THE THREE PILLARS

THE TREE OF LIFE HAS THREE PILLARS, EACH OF WHICH IS ESSENTIAL FOR THE MAINTENANCE OF BALANCE. THE CENTRAL COLUMN REPRESENTS CONSCIOUSNESS, WHILE THE SIDE COLUMNS REPRESENT THE ACTIVE (RIGHT-HAND) AND PASSIVE (LEFT-HAND) PRINCIPLES. THERE IS A TENDENCY TO ASSUME THAT ACTIVE EQUALS "STRONG" AND PASSIVE EQUALS "WEAK", BUT THE TREE OF LIFE ASCRIBES EQUAL POWER AND IMPORTANCE TO BOTH COLUMNS. AS LIFE ON EARTH IS BASED ON DUALITY OR, MORE ACCURATELY, CONTRAST, THE TWO OUTER PILLARS ARE A VITAL PART OF THE PATTERN OF EXISTENCE. WITHOUT THEM NO CHOICES COULD BE MADE AND NO GROWTH EXPERIENCED. MOST HUMANS ARE SLIGHTLY IMBALANCED TOWARD ONE SIDE OR THE OTHER, AND THIS WILL SHOW IN THEIR BEHAVIOUR AND LIFESTYLE. THE PHRASE "TO FEEL CENTRED" REFERS TO BEING BALANCED AT TIFERET ON THE MIDDLE COLUMN.

ABOVE Wells Cathedral, in England, is a great example of a church built in the Middle Ages, in that it features two side towers and a central entrance. These represent the balance of masculine and feminine required to experience divinity.

RIGHT Raising our consciousness out of the ego can best be achieved by experiencing challenges or adventures we might never have undertaken before. We reveal our true self, and our strengths and weaknesses in times of crisis.

The three columns are the Pillar of Consciousness, at the centre, the Pillar of Action on the right and the Pillar of Receptivity on the left.

THE PILLAR OF CONSCIOUSNESS

The Pillar of Consciousness runs from Malkhut to Keter and represents focus and temptation. A person who is aware of his or her self stands at Tiferet on this column with information coming in from all the paths around him or her. In front, on the journey, is the black hole of Da'at, which signifies either transformation or the abyss, and behind is the Sefira of Yesod, representing the ego. The goal of the journey is Keter, the crown, or the place of

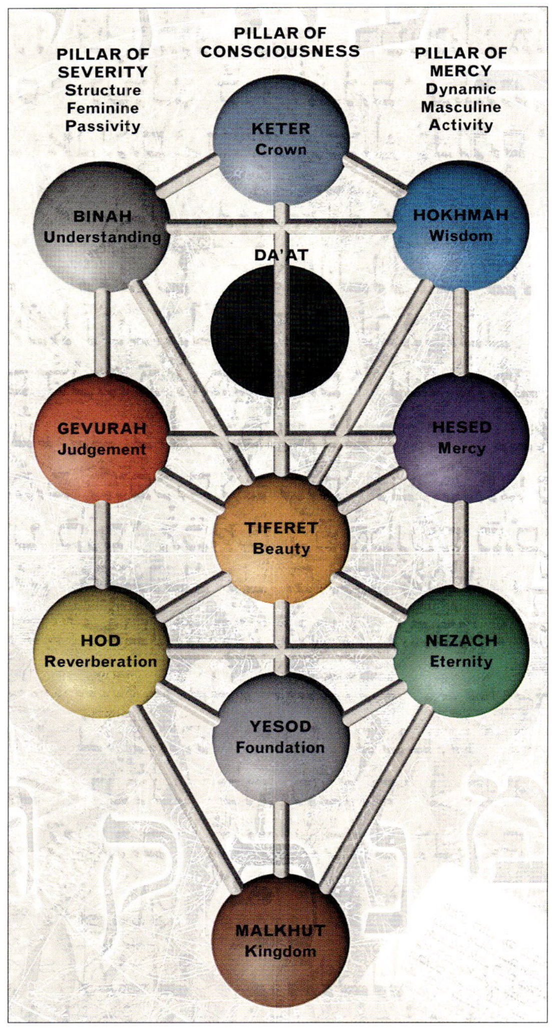

ABOVE The Kabbalist aims to live on the central column, blending the two side pillars so as not become imbalanced. The right-hand pillar is traditionally active and masculine, and the left is passive and feminine.

access to the Holy One, and at the other end of the pillar is Malkhut, or physical reality. Human beings rarely reside in Tiferet, holding the reins of the other Sefirot in perfect balance but, rather, are over-balanced to one side or the other, with the result that their lives feel over-pressured or under-achieving.

THE PILLAR OF ACTION

The right-hand pillar is the Pillar of Action. It is also the masculine principle of the Tree of Life and the place of light, giving, creativity, generosity and mercy. Someone who has too much emphasis on the right-hand pillar could be constantly doing without thinking, over-helping others, a workaholic, controlling and manipulative. The Sefirot on the active side of the Tree of Life are Nezach, which embraces artistic or creative talent, creativity, sensuality and sexuality, and is ruled by the planet Venus; Hesed, which represents loving kindness, mercy and expansion and is ruled by the planet Jupiter; and Hokhmah, which represents wisdom, inspiration, revelation and revolution and is ruled by the planet Uranus. According to Kabbalistic teaching, it is a masculine principle to give, and many people find their life out of balance on the right-hand pillar, either by over-controlling or by over-giving to family and friends. Mothers, for example, often over-give through coping with work and children without taking time out for rest. Imbalance on the Tree can lead to physical sickness.

THE PILLAR OF RECEPTIVITY

The left-hand pillar is known as the Pillar of Receptivity and represents the feminine principle of the Tree of Life. It is the place of night, strength, darkness, discernment, judgement, thought, response and passivity. Someone who is out of balance, with too much emphasis on the left-hand pillar, could be hermit-like, over-intellectual, severe, cruel and inactive. The Sefirot on the receptive side of the Tree of Life are Hod, which represents theory, intelligence and thought and is ruled by the planet Mercury; Gevurah represents discipline and judgement, and is ruled by the planet Mars; and Binah represents understanding, boundaries and structure, and is ruled by the planet Saturn.

In ancient days, the feminine pillar was linked with evil, which reflected Jewish attitudes toward women. More modern interpretations consider this negativity as the vital process of establishing boundaries and judicious use of the word "no". According to Kabbalistic teaching, it is the feminine principle to be passive, and many people who allow their parents, boss or partner to rule their life may be too focused on the left-hand pillar. A balance between giving and receiving is all-important for maintaining good health.

BELOW This early 18th-century Dutch painting of the plan of Solomon's Temple shows the four courtyards, each one representing a level of Jacob's Ladder. The outer court (Asiyyah) was open to all, the Court of the Women (Yezirah) was open only to Jews, the Court of the Men and the place of animal sacrifice (Beriah) was open only to men, and the sanctuary (Azilut) was only available to the priesthood.

SOLOMON'S TEMPLE

When the Israelites had found and conquered the Promised Land, as related in the Book of Exodus, they were able to build a static temple instead of carrying the Tabernacle with them on their travels. Solomon's Temple was built on exactly the same structure as the Tabernacle, representing both the Tree of Life and Jacob's Ladder. The Tree was represented by the great pillars on either side of the central door, and the ladder by the great courts within the temple. The Second Temple, built by Herod the Great, which was in existence at the time of Jesus of Nazareth, was built on the same design. The outer court, which became known as the Court of the Gentiles, signified Asiyyah, the physical world; the Court of the Women, Yezirah, the psychological world; the Court of the Men represented Beriah, the spiritual world; and the inner sanctuary, or Holy of Holies, represented Azilut, the divine world.

Jacob's Ladder

EACH OF THE FOUR WORLDS HAS ITS OWN TREE OF LIFE, AND THESE LINK TO FORM A PATTERN. FOR MANY CENTURIES, ALL FOUR WORLDS WERE SHOWN WITHIN THE LEVELS OF THE YEZIRATIC TREE OF LIFE – PHYSICAL BELOW THE LIMINAL LINE; PSYCHOLOGICAL BETWEEN THE LIMINAL AND THE SOUL TRIAD LINE; SPIRITUAL BETWEEN THE SOUL TRIAD LINE AND THE SUPERNAL TRIAD LINE; AND DIVINE ABOVE THE SUPERNAL TRIAD LINE. THEY WERE ALSO SHOWN WITHIN A COMPLEX SERIES OF DIAGRAMS THAT VARY FROM TRADITION TO TRADITION AND WERE OFTEN MORE CONFUSING THAN REVEALING. JACOB'S LADDER CLEARLY SHOWS THE INTERWEAVING OF FOUR DIFFERENT LEVELS AND, WHILE IT APPEARS COMPLEX AT FIRST SIGHT, OPERATES ON A SIMPLE, LOGICAL BASIS THAT MAKES IT EASY TO COMPREHEND WHEN THE PRINCIPLES OF THE TREE OF LIFE ITSELF ARE UNDERSTOOD.

ABOVE The Tree of the Soul, a design by a 16th-century German Kabbalist, showing the four worlds. Masonic symbolism – the triangle, the all-seeing eye of God, and the sword – are all evident, even though many people date the start of Freemasonry only to the 17th century.

RIGHT Jacob wrestling with the angel (Genesis 32:24). After this, Jacob was given the name 'Israel' meaning "one who struggles with God." Kabbalah would consider all spiritual seekers to be either Children of Israel or Israelites according to the level of their development.

Jacob's Ladder vanished from the public domain after the teachings of Isaac Luria became the most prominent aspect of Kabbalah. It re-emerged in the 1970s with the development of the pre-Lurianic Toledano tradition. Exactly how it was devised prior to the 16th century is not clear, as no clear evidence remains, but the principle of 11 concentric circles (the 10 Sefirot and Da'at on the extended Tree) is a repeated spiritual symbol, noticeable in places such as the great labyrinth at Chartres Cathedral. The Tabernacle shown in the Book of Exodus lays out the principles of the ladder clearly.

BASIC PRINCIPLES

The Ladder depicts the relationship between the four worlds, or levels of existence. The four levels are Azilut, the divine world; Beriah, the spiritual world; Yezirah, the world of forms (or of the psyche); and Asiyyah, the physical world. Each one is interwoven

with the other, demonstrating that each human has a physical body, a psyche and a spirit, and is in touch with the divine. At the base is the physical world, which includes the workings of the human or animal body, such as the bone structure, nervous system and skin. This is interwoven with the psyche so that the central point of the physical body locks in with the base of the psyche and the crown of the physical body locks in with the centre of the psyche as well as with the base of the spiritual body. Each world interleaves in the same way and, to the experienced Kabbalist, reading the ladder is like reading a pictorial alphabet such as hieroglyphics.

HUMANITY AND THE FOUR WORLDS

According to Kabbalistic teaching, humans are the only living creatures who can access all four worlds of Jacob's Ladder. Humans can contact the spiritual realm when they are balanced and focused in Tiferet. Most psychics work from the Hod of Yezirah, being in touch with lower energies – discarnate humans, angelic beings and devas (fairies). Archangels live in the Beriatic world, and animals live in the Asiyyatic and lower Yeziratic worlds.

God exists in all four worlds, and that is why humanity is unique in being able to reflect God back to God. Everything is divine in origin, and everything from the basest rock to the highest archangel reflects

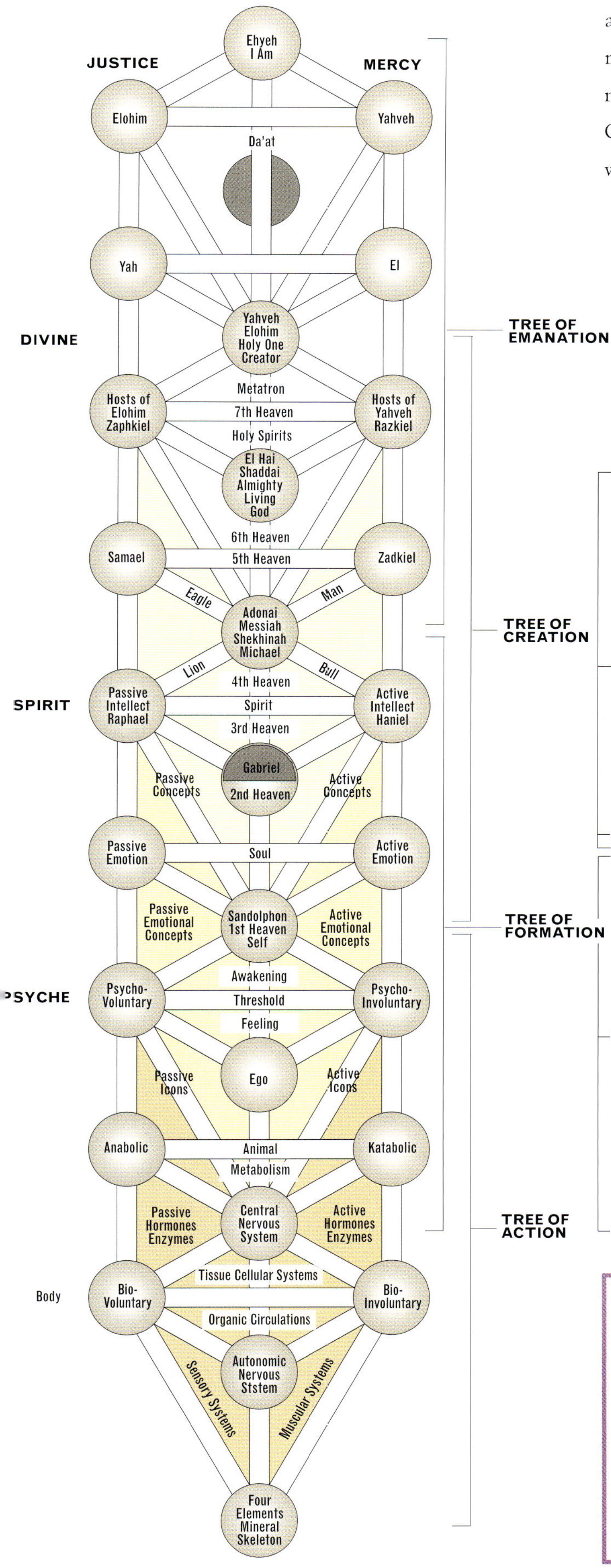

an aspect of God. Only humanity has the ability to reflect back on all levels. That is what gives us so much possibility and responsibility. As children of God we are co-creators with God; our every thought, word and deed has outcomes throughout the universe.

FAR LEFT Jacob's ladder demonstrates how the four worlds of Creation weave together. It is a map of the universe and also of human development. We humans can access every part of the ladder through consciousness while incarnate. No other creature, including the archangels, can do this. While appearing very complex, the ladder is easily understood with the application of basic Kabbalistic principles.

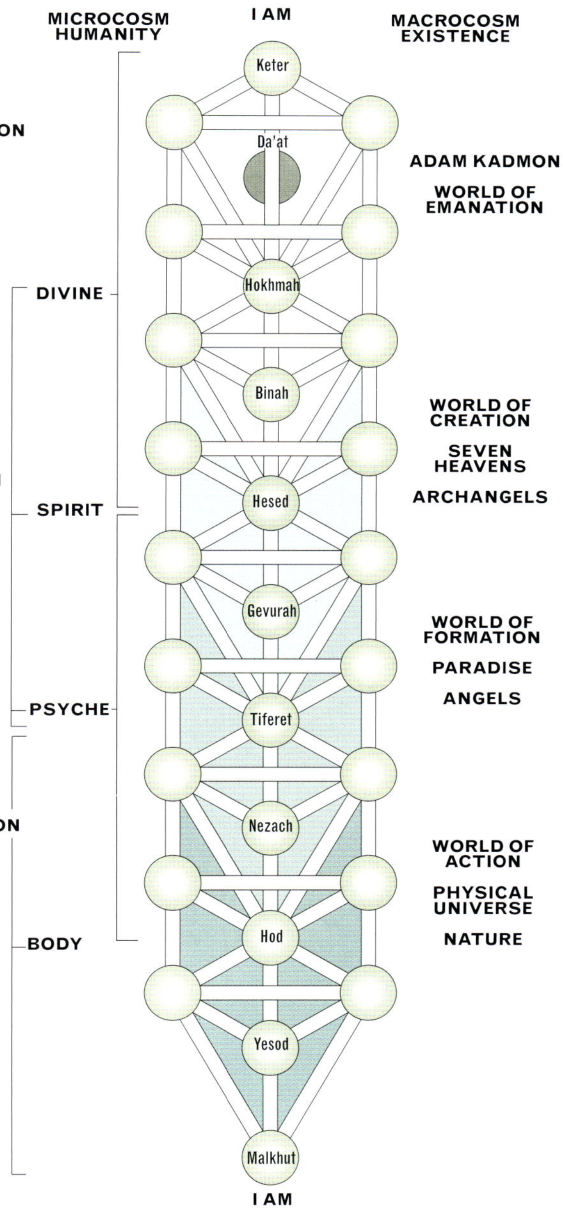

LEFT The Fifth Tree, also known as the Great Tree, is comprised of the ten Sefirot that run up the central column of Jacob's Ladder. This Tree forms the structure of the "The Lord's Prayer", as taught by Jesus of Nazareth, beginning with "Our Father" at the Keter of Keters and finishing with "Deliver us from evil" at the Malkhut of Malkhuts. The final phrase in the prayer was added by St Paul.

THE FIFTH TREE

The ten Sefirot of the Tree of Life can form one great tree up the central column of Jacob's Ladder. Modern Christian Kabbalists, who believe the four Gospels each represent one of the four worlds of Jacob's Ladder, teach that this is what John the Baptist means, when he says in Matthew 3:3: "Prepare ye the way of the Lord, make his paths straight."

AZILUT

AZILUT IS THE WORLD OF FIRE; OF PURE EMANATION AND DIVINITY AND THE CLOSEST WORLD TO GOD. IT IS A WORLD THAT IS INEXPLICABLE AND INCOMPREHENSIBLE, CONTAINING THE SEEDS OF ALL CREATION. IN THIS WORLD THERE IS NO TIME, SEXUALITY OR FORM. IT IS HERE THAT ADAM KADMON, THE DIVINE MAN, RESIDES, AS WELL AS THE ARCHANGEL METATRON, THE FIRST PERFECT HUMAN BEING. THE MALKHUT OF AZILUT IS CONSIDERED THE GATEWAY TO THE DIVINE WORLD FOR HUMAN BEINGS. AZILUT IS WHERE ALL HUMAN SOULS ORIGINATE AND BELONG. IT IS THE YEARNING TO GO HOME TO THIS WORLD THAT IMPELS US TO SEEK SPIRITUAL INSPIRATION, BUT WHEN A SOUL IS VERY YOUNG IT MAY LOSE MUCH OF ITS CONNECTION WITH THE DIVINE THROUGH THE RIGOURS OF EXISTENCE AND THE EXCITEMENT OF PHYSICAL SENSATION.

ABOVE The Egyptian god Anubis was often depicted supervising the weighing of the human soul when the departed were brought to the hall of the dead. With the advent of Christianity, this task was deputed to the archangel Michael, weighing souls here, in an alterpiece dating back to 1200.

RIGHT This 17th-century image of Jacob's Ladder shows that the mysticism of the ladder leading to the divine world of Azilut, though hidden to the majority of Kabbalists, was still being revealed to the serious seeker.

The Malkhut of Azilut is the Sefira of the aspect of divinity known as "the Lord", and it is also the place of the Messiah. It is also what Jesus is referring to when he speaks of the Kingdom of God. 'Malkhut' means "kingdom" in Hebrew.

This Sefira is the gateway to the divine world and the highest state of consciousness to which humanity can aspire while incarnate. For most humans, accessing the plane of this Sefira is a rare occurrence. When it is achieved, the aspirant is in full control of his or her psyche, spiritually centred and directly in touch with the divine. However, most humans can hold that level for only a few minutes at most. A Messiah (in Kabbalistic terms, the person currently alive who is the Anointed of God) could access that plane of consciousness for much of their life and be a direct channel of divine will.

Jesus of Nazareth speaks of the Kingdom of God throughout the four Gospels, referring simultaneously to his own ability to access that exalted state of mind and also emphasizing how it is accessible to all those who are spiritually clear and connected with "the Father" (the divine world). The Kingdom of God is the level that Merkabah riders are attempting to reach.

LEFT Fire is associated with the world of Azilut, and contact with this world will burn – and even kill – the uninitiated who try to access it without suitable protection or wisdom. It is from fire that all light and life emanates, and each one of us at the deepest level consists of pure light – as a spark of the Divine Human, Adam Kadmon.

METATRON

The great archangel Metatron is unique in the heavenly ranks. He is said to be the first fully perfected human being, Enoch, who ascended without physical death to take the place of the Tiferet of Azilut. As such, Enoch is also placed at the crown of Beriah and is therefore the prince of all the cherubim and archangels. Metatron is also known as the Prince of the Presence, the Teacher of Teachers, and the Regent of God. According to Kabbalistic legend, Metatron, being unique among the angels, is also two archangelic beings in one. He is also the archangel Sandalfon, who is placed at the Malkhut of Beriah. Sandalfon is so tall that he extends the full length of Jacob's Ladder and makes wreaths of prayers to pass on to the Holy One. Any prayer that is directed toward God or toward the angels, saints or sages for intercession, is collected by the relevant power and passed on to Sandalfon. Because the being who is both Sandalfon and Metatron was once human, the prayers are passed up to the Holy One with a deeper level of understanding than could come from an angel who had never experienced the desires of humanity.

TOUCHING THE DIVINE

In ancient days, before cities containing millions of people existed, there was always a spiritual aspect to any life, whether it was through religion or the observation of the cycles of nature. So-called primitive tribes and societies trained their youngsters in the values of discipline, hunting and both astronomy and astrology. Boys and girls experienced rites of passage at important stages of their growth and were expected to engage with some form of deity or spirit for protection and guidance.

Nowadays, with media and Internet distractions and secular lifestyles, much of humanity is not encouraged to seek the divine. The growth of fundamentalism in both Christianity and Islam is often more cultural than spiritual, but esoteric traditions, including Kabbalah, will always exist to provide pathways to the divine for those who are seeking contact with higher worlds.

BELOW A 14th-century Italian fresco depicting Jesus' entry into Jerusalem on Palm Sunday, from the story of the Passion of Christ. A Messiah is someone who has risen to the level of consciousness that embraces the three higher worlds of Yezirah, Beriah and Azilut.

THE TREASURE HOUSE OF SOULS

Kabbalah teaches that all human souls come from a specific limb or organ of Adam Kadmon, the primordial man. This is to indicate that each human soul has a particular purpose throughout its many lives. According to the Zohar, all human souls, before their first incarnation, reside as divine sparks in the Treasure House of Souls. This is the soul triad area of Azilut. Just like a human female baby's ovaries already contain all the eggs that she will carry throughout her reproductive life, all the human souls that are still awaiting their first incarnation in the future reside in the Treasure House.

Beriah

Beriah is the world of air and creation. It is here that the archangels live, and it is here that great concepts are born. Beriah is the realm of pure mind – a timeless world of potential that interweaves with Azilut and also with Yezirah. It is in this world where duality begins: the concept of up and down, black and white, and good and evil. An example of this world would be where a human being might conceive that he or she would like to help humanity and feel a drive to do so, but has not worked out exactly *how* he or she could do that. The great archetypes exist here too: the Great Horse, the Great Dog, the Great Lion and the perfect *ideas* of these beasts.

ABOVE Archangels on the crypt ceiling at Montemaria Abbey, Burgusio Bolzano, Italy. Kabbalah teaches that neither angels nor archangels have feet – as they are not human and never stand on the physical world. Their wings are depictions of the aura of light that surrounds them.

RIGHT The angel of the Annunciation appearing to the Virgin Mary. This is the archangel Gabriel, who is placed at the Da'at of Yezirah and the Yesod of Beriah – the places where spirit communicates to the human psyche. Gabriel is sacred to Monday, the Moon, homes, domestic life and pets.

Beriah is the home of ultimate cosmic good and evil. These are principles that embody unending creation and unending destruction. At this level, all processes are clear, pure and transpersonal. Beriah carries the basic principles of duality, and these exist so that the cycles of life can exist, reliant as they are on growth, reproduction, death and decay. All of Beriah is uncompromising principle.

Understanding Good and Evil

To many humans the destruction of a town by an earthquake or flood is evil, with many who believe in God wondering how such cruelty could be allowed. However, Kabbalah teaches that the natural forces of destruction and creation are neutral and simply necessary for planets, solar systems and universes to go about their business. What causes the destruction of an earthquake may be the creation of a new mountain. It could be said that it is pure, cosmic evil that is the driving force behind the rotting of a dead plant into compost from which new life can emerge in the form of a new plant. It could also be said that it is pure, cosmic good that animates a parasite. Both forces are impartial, and it is only our human interpretation that gives them the labels good or bad. Where human free will – or lack of it – comes in is when we choose to live in an area that is known to be geographically unstable, or do not (or cannot) give the matter a thought.

LUCIFER

In legends of the Creation, the greatest of the angelic beings was Lucifer, known as the Son of Morning. He was jealous of Adam, the first man, and challenged him to a contest to see who was the greatest. The Holy One asked both beings to name the creatures. Lucifer was unable to think in such a lateral way, and Adam won the competition. Lucifer then decided that he would rather rule in hell than serve in heaven and became an outcast. Lucifer is Satan, the tempter, trying to obstruct humans on their path of growth. This still makes him God's greatest servant, for Kabbalah teaches that all humans must be tested to prove their mettle on the way back to the heavens.

LEFT Gustave Doré's depiction of Satan vanquished. Satan, or Lucifer, was the highest of the archangels, but his refusal to acknowledge humanity as God's greatest creation led to his fall from heaven. It is said he preferred to rule in hell than serve in heaven.

ANGELIC RANKS

Angels are the servants of archangels, and archangels are the servants of God. There are ranks of angels even higher than archangels, called cherubim (these are nothing like the cute little cherubs on Christmas cards). Cherubim come in three ranks: Seraphim, Wheels and Thrones, and they live in the higher realms of Beriah, interacting with Azilut. The energy of an archangel is similar to the Sun. Planets such as Earth are in the care of an angel. Archangels exist in Beriah, and angels exist in Yezirah. Angels can be of all different sizes, from a flower fairy (or deva) to the angel of a specific country or planet and, being Yeziratic beings, can appear to humans in many guises.

As humans are children of God and angels are servants of God, humans have the power and the ability to summon the angels and the energy equivalent of archangels. However, this must be done responsibly and carefully. Kabbalah teaches that angels and archangels are not beings to be called on for comfort as if they were friends, but great celestial beings whose duty is to ensure that the great cycles of life endure.

According to Kabbalistic teachings, angels do not have free will. They are created solely for a specific purpose and do not engage in any other activity. An angel of love is always an angel of love, an angel of creativity is always an angel of creativity and so forth. Kabbalah teaches that such focus is vital in the running of universes, as a moment's lack of concentration could mean the end of a galaxy.

BELOW This image of the Dome of the Rock, sacred both to Islam and Judaism, shows all four worlds of creation – the physical landscape, clouds made from water and air, the air itself and the light of the Sun. It is only through the vehicle of air (spirit) that humanity can see clearly.

YEZIRAH

YEZIRAH IS THE WORLD GENERALLY KNOWN AS THE TREE OF LIFE. IT IS THE WORLD OF WATER AND THE PLACE WHERE THINGS CALLED FORTH (AZILUT) AND CREATED (BERIAH) BY THE HOLY ONE TAKE ON SPECIFIC QUALITIES AND CHARACTERISTICS. THE GREAT HORSE OF CREATION BECOMES THE DIFFERENT BREEDS OF HORSE – SHETLAND PONY, LIPIZZANER, HAFLINGER, GREY, BLACK OR CHESTNUT. IN YEZIRAH, TIME BEGINS. YEZIRAH IS THE WORLD OF THE HUMAN EMOTIONS AND OF THE LOVES AND FEARS THAT WE HAVE CREATED WITHIN OURSELVES. IT IS NOT REAL, AS IN PHYSICALLY PRESENT, BUT IS NONETHELESS VERY POWERFUL. THE INTERNET AND TELEVISION ARE BOTH YEZIRATIC; THEY JUST TRANSMIT IMAGES BUT, FOR THE VIEWER, THE CRISIS IN A TV SOAP OPERA MAY BE MORE EMOTIONALLY DRAINING THAN AN IMAGE FROM THE NEWS.

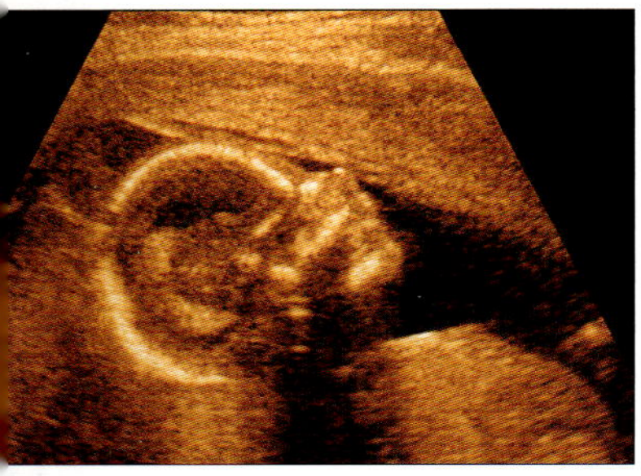

ABOVE An ultrasound scan of a human baby. The soul, which exists in the Yeziratic world, does not come fully into the mother's body until birth. It will connect at the point of quickening to establish the link essential to life, but should anything go wrong with the physical vehicle, the soul does not die; it simply remains in Yezirah until a stronger body can support it.

RIGHT Three worlds meeting. At the pivotal point of the three lower worlds, the human being is in control of the body, centred in the psyche and in contact with spirit. This is the place referred to in the Bible as "the Kingdom of Heaven". This is the place where meditation is achieved and free will can be accessed – and where grace can be perceived. Miracles happen here.

The tree of the psyche is a blueprint of a perfect human being, linked above to the spiritual and divine worlds and below to the physical body. Most of our great fears and desires exist in Yezirah, but our belief in them can rule our life.

THE CREATION OF LIFE

When we are born, our souls descend into life from the Keter of the Yeziratic Tree (which is also the Malkhut of Azilut and the Tiferet of Beriah), down the Lightning Flash to Malkhut, and then climb back up the Tree as we learn and develop as humans. As all the worlds are intertwined, creation takes place at all levels simultaneously. The Keter of Yezirah represents conception, with Hokhmah as the spark of life connecting and inspiring the first growth. Binah then adds structure – defining what kind of life we are – cat, sheep or human. Da'at is the place of spontaneous abortion in the first three months of conception; if the foetus survives, then it begins to grow in earnest at Hesed, and begins moving inside the mother's body. This is known as "quickening".

At Gevurah, the forming body is honed and defined again to consolidate its bone structure, health and strength; at Tiferet, where the spiritual, psychological and physical worlds meet, the baby's lungs develop, making it able to sustain life should it be born early. At Nezach the baby's brain is

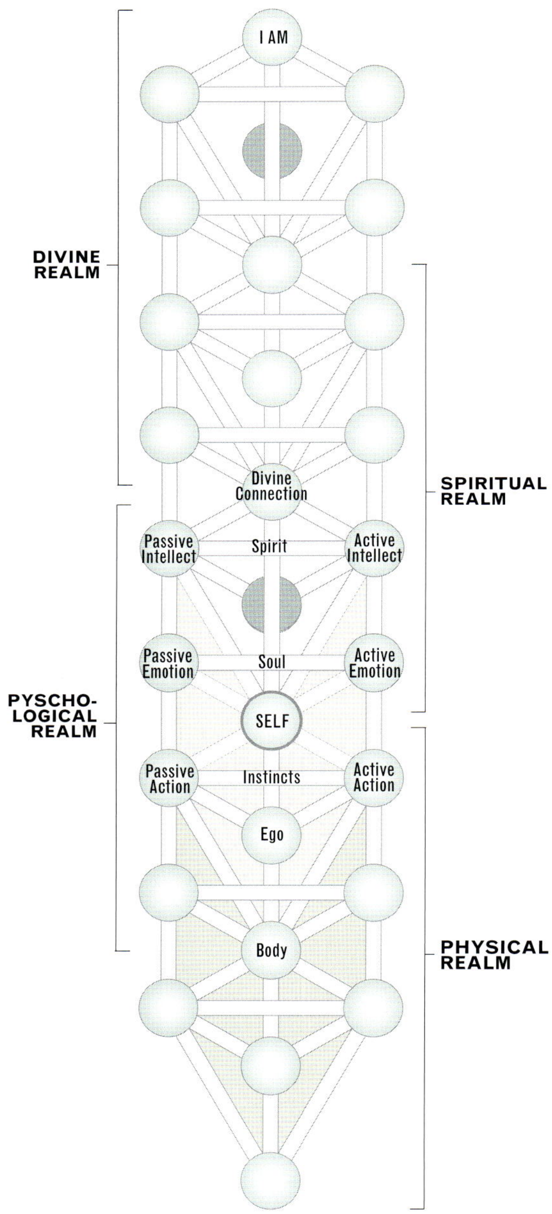

growing, developing billions of new nerve cells; its bone marrow is producing its own red blood cells, and the baby will double and then triple its size. At Hod, muscle mass and fat stores consolidate, and the baby is sensitive to sound and light, with eyes that open and shut. At Yesod, the final finishing touches are added, including the process of storing iron in the liver and the first potential functioning of the bowels – and the baby "drops" in the uterus to present itself ready for birth at Malkhut.

THE SOUL

Each human soul is unique and exists both before and after physical life. It is the soul that learns to understand the deeper issues of right and wrong, and it is the soul that dictates a person's destiny. The soul and the spirit differ in that the soul is uniquely personal to each human being while also being connected to the Beriatic world of the transpersonal – the collective destiny of humanity. The spirit is wholly transpersonal and a specific impulse of the creative force that overrides any personal feeling or emotion. The ideal is to blend the two levels, enabling us to remain in contact with our own concepts of justice and mercy and make conscious decisions. On the Tree of Life, the soul is placed in the triad between Gevurah, Tiferet and Hesed.

THE KINGDOM OF HEAVEN

The word Malkhut means "kingdom" in Hebrew, and the Malkhut of Beriah (the Tiferet of Yezirah) is known as the Kingdom of Heaven. Jesus referred to it 32 times in the Gospel of Matthew, using it in stories and parables, including the declaration that we must become like an innocent child to enter the Kingdom of Heaven. He was making it clear that this kingdom is a state of mind; a place where we are not ruled by social and psychological habits and regulations. It is also the pivotal point between the three lower worlds and the place from which we can aspire to reach the Kingdom of God.

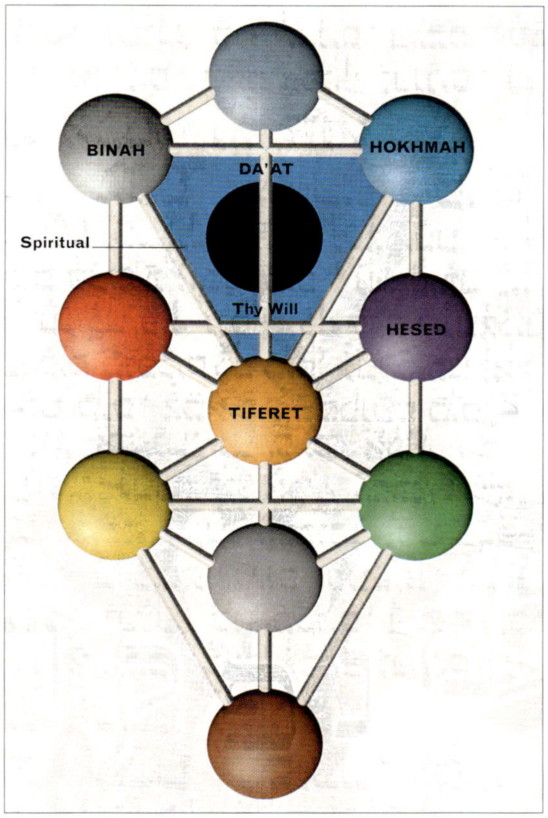

LEFT Our psychological make-up is complex, with deep conditioning on both emotional and cultural levels influencing our every decision. The Tiferet of the Yeziratic Tree receives information from body, soul, spirit and all the outside influences that have shaped our everyday life, from our religion to our first experience of rejection. Over-focusing on painful or pleasurable conditions in our life can make us lose contact with Tiferet – and the Kingdom of Heaven.

BELOW Yezirah is the world of water – feelings, emotions and thoughts that can be easily swayed just as water can be agitated by movement from above or below. Learning to "swim with the flow" is helpful in order to ride the storms of life.

FREE WILL

People do not always use free will for good purposes. Men and women who believe it is their duty to inspire others to kill in the service of a deity are often acting from the soul triad. Their concept of justice and mercy is out of balance, and they are allowing themselves to be over-influenced by the severity of philosophical or religious training in the side triads of Gevurah, Binah, Tiferet or Hesed, Hokhmah, Tiferet. These are the triads that are concerned with philosophy and religion, which, if too rigid, will affect the concept of truth and freedom.

ASIYYAH

ASIYYAH IS THE PHYSICAL WORLD OF EARTH, THE WORLD THAT ADAM AND EVE ENTERED WHEN THEY "PUT ON COATS OF SKIN". WE THINK OF IT AS A VERY STRONG AND SOLID PLACE, BUT KABBALAH TEACHES THAT IT IS THE MOST FRAGILE OF ALL THE WORLDS. THIS IS BECAUSE PHYSICAL DEATH IS ALWAYS CLOSE AT HAND, AND IT CAN DESTROY THE PHYSICAL VEHICLE, WHEREAS THE PSYCHE, SPIRIT AND DIVINE PRINCIPLE ARE CONSTANT. ASIYYAH IS THE FURTHEST WORLD FROM DIVINITY AND IS SUBJECT TO A GREATER NUMBER OF LAWS THAN THE OTHER WORLDS BECAUSE OF ITS FRAGILITY. ALL THAT EXISTS ARE THE EFFECTS OF THE THOUGHTS, BELIEFS OR CAUSES THAT HAVE PREVIOUSLY BEEN CONCEIVED IN BERIAH AND FORMED IN YEZIRAH, BOTH BY GOD AND BY HUMANITY. KABBALAH TEACHES THAT THOUGHT CREATES REALITY.

ABOVE We experience the physical world of Asiyyah through our senses. A walk in the woods would not be complete without the sight of trees, the feel of the ground beneath our feet and the sounds around us.

Science can now prove that life consists of vibration and that there is actually more space and movement in Asiyyah than we can possibly contemplate. Each component in a human body is surrounded by space and each one is, in itself, extremely fragile.

THE TREE OF THE BODY

Asiyyah is the Tree of the human body. It is, effectively, a diagram of how our DNA operates. Beginning with the skeleton at Malkhut, the tree features the nervous system in the triad of Malkhut, Hod, Yesod and the muscular system in the triad of Malkhut, Nezach, Yesod. The membranes around both are represented in the paths between Malkhut and Hod and Malkhut and Nezach. Hod represents the communication systems of the body and Nezach the motility systems. In the triad between Yesod, Hod and Nezach sit the pulmonary and lymphatic systems, and the tissues and cells are represented in the Tiferet, Nezach, Hod triad. Anabolic/catabolic processes and the metabolism

RIGHT Touching three worlds – the Celestial Ladder from *De Nova Logica*. Human beings need to be fully "grounded" in the physical world and "centred" in the psychological world to be able to experience higher levels safely.

are the responsibility of the triad between Gevurah, Hesed and Tiferet, with negative hormones and enzymes in the triad below Gevurah and positive hormones and enzymes in the triad below Hesed.

Gevurah, Binah, Tiferet is the area of negative ions, while Hokhmah, Hesed, Tiferet is the triad of positive ions. In the Tiferet, Binah, Hokhmah triad of the body, the psyche and body are inextricably linked, so that information from the body can filter through its Da'at into the Yesod of the psyche, alerting the human as to whether all is physically well or not.

TOUCHING THREE WORLDS

Each world or level in Kabbalah emerges from the centre of the one above it, so that there is an interpenetration of all four worlds – emanation, creation, formation and action. Human beings can perceive all four worlds if they are balanced and present at the Kingdom of Heaven – the Tiferet of Yezirah, the psychological world. Once a student of Kabbalah becomes focused at Tiferet, he or she becomes conscious of the soul level, which means that life is observed from a completely new viewpoint. What had seemed very personal can now be seen from a wider perspective and, with the input of the higher worlds filtered through the individual soul, the life's journey and perhaps even its destiny become apparent.

PERFECTING A SPECIES

Many beliefs and traditions hold that animals retain an individual identity after death or that humans can reincarnate in animal form. Kabbalah subscribes to neither belief. It teaches that each animal belongs intrinsically to a group soul – for example, the soul of Dog or the soul of Horse. Each animal returns to that group identity, which is perfecting itself just as Adam Kadmon is doing. Kabbalah emphasizes that all of God's creations are intended to perfect themselves and therefore do not reincarnate across species, as this would blur the great picture rather than refining it. Once a creature is perfected, it is entirely possible that it may voluntarily become extinct on planet Earth, as it has no further need to develop itself.

This is a kinder principle than many people believe, for if a pet animal retained its individuality, it could miss its owner on dying and be lonely. However, some psychic Kabbalists teach that once an owner is in deep meditation or discarnate, he or she can contact the individual essence of their former pet and the two will recognize each other. When the human is discarnate, that part of the animal soul can even separate out to spend time with its former owner, but it will then return to its own soul-source unless it is due to reincarnate.

ABOVE Humans frequently attempt to perfect different species. Hundreds of different types of dogs, cats, cattle and horses are now bred for specific characteristics, from beauty through strength to giving maximum levels of food production. However, such selective breeding often produces as many flaws as it does improvements.

REINCARNATION

The principle of reincarnation is integral to Kabbalistic teaching. Humans are said to make four basic journeys over many hundreds of lifetimes. The first is the descent into physical matter to learn how to live in the world; the second is the awakening of spiritual awareness; the third is to pass on what has been learned, and the fourth is the final return to God. In each lifetime different lessons are learned, but the system is fundamentally fair in that all humanity has an equal opportunity to develop over many different incarnations. To a Kabbalist, the idea that God would give only one life, which might end in childhood or take place in an area where there was no opportunity for growth, would be unthinkable.

BELOW Rather than believe in reincarnation, Kabbalists believe that animals are reborn into a group identity, for example, the soul of Horse. In this way the group, or species, can try to perfect itself.

Kabbalah and Astrology

It is only in the last two centuries that astrology has been separated from the study of astronomy and derided as fantasy. The Greek word *magi*, used for the three wise men who were directed to the infant Jesus, means "astrologer priest". Sun-sign astrology was made popular by the press in 1930 when the *Sunday Express* published an article by R. H. Naylor about the birth of the British princess Margaret. The newspaper's sales increased dramatically, so he was asked to write regular astrology columns of relevance for everyone. As this is impossible without extreme simplification of astrology, he invented sun-sign columns, which spread like wildfire throughout the world. There had been popular astrological almanacs dating back as far as 1468, but these did not use the Sun alone to determine details of people's lives and fortunes.

ABOVE The core beliefs of astrology prevalent in most of the ancient world are epitomized in the Hermetic maxim "as above, so below". Those who practise astrology believe the positions of certain celestial bodies (chiefly the Sun, Moon, and the planets) influence people's personality traits, important events in their lives, physical characteristics, and to some extent their destiny.

RIGHT The main links between Kabbalah and astrology are shown in the correspondences between the planets, sun signs and the paths of the Tree of Life.

The 12 signs of the zodiac, the 10 planets and the recently-discovered "planetoids" all fit on to the Tree of Life. Astrology is a Yeziratic concept only; a human being's astrological chart is a blueprint that can be overcome at any time by the use of free will. However, placing your astrological chart on to the Tree of Life is very helpful in seeing where potential conflicts and opportunities exist in your life.

Planets on the Tree

The ten planets of the solar system fit neatly on to the Tree of Life, with the Earth or Ascendant at Malkhut; the Moon, with its regularly repeating 28-day cycle at Yesod; Mercury at Hod; Venus at Nezach; and the Sun at Tiferet. The old proverb "nothing new under the Sun" is a Kabbalistic saying referring to the vegetable and animal levels of existence below Tiferet, where life repeats and recycles itself. It is only from Tiferet onward that free will can create new experience. Mars rules the Sefira of Gevurah, with Jupiter at Hesed. Pluto represents Da'at, with Saturn at Binah and Uranus at Hokhmah. Neptune signifies Keter.

Until the discovery of the outer planets of Uranus, Neptune and Pluto, other zodiacal representations were placed at Hokhmah, Keter and Da'at.

Modern astronomers have demoted Pluto to the status of a 'dwarf planet', and claim to have discovered other planets – or planetoids – that are larger. However, Da'at is a mysterious, mostly

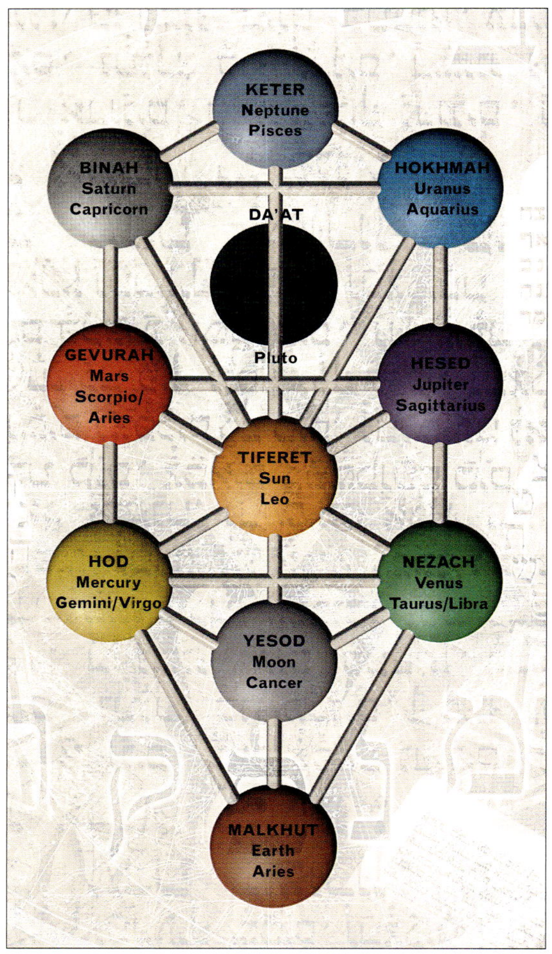

undiscovered place, so it is unlikely that any "normal" planet could represent it. At the moment, Pluto appears to fit the scheme simply because it has an erratic orbit that moves in and out of the solar system, so representing the link between the Yeziratic world and the realm of Beriah.

Pluto was discovered in 1930 and takes 248 years to orbit the Sun so, although astrologers can assess its effects on humanity through its orbit as observed already, the full picture can only be educated guess-work. The other recently-discovered planetoids at the same distance from Earth as Pluto have not been observed in their cycles but, as they would move approximately three degrees in the average human being's lifetime their effect on individual lives is, at the moment, incalculable.

ABOVE Z'ev ben Shimon Halevi's cosmic clock outlines the principles of astrology, and shows the planets and their rulership in active or passive roles. The outermost ring, with its dark and light halves, refers to day and night. The Ascendent is observed on the left, the Descendent on the right with dusk.

THE ASTROLOGICAL SIGNS ON THE TREE

Each of the twelve zodiacal signs are represented in one of the triads of the Tree of Life. The two great triads of the upper and lower faces of the Yeziratic Tree are ruled by Leo and Cancer – which rule fatherhood and motherhood – and the rest demonstrate the characteristics of the triad where they are placed. Understanding the signs and what they represent makes it much easier to understand the Sefirot, paths and triads of the Tree of Life.

A good example would be the triad of Gevurah, Tiferet, Hod, which is the place of deep negative personal emotions such as fear, anger and hatred. This is ruled by Scorpio, the astrological sign which represents these emotions together with paranoia and self-destructive tendencies. It is the positive aspect of Scorpio of being able to see through all dishonesty and illusion and focus on spiritual growth rather than on negativity, which is needed to transform the negative aspects of this triad.

The corresponding triad of Tiferet, Hesed, Nezach is ruled by Pisces. Like Scorpio, Pisces is a water sign, concerned with emotion. This triad represents deep inner positive emotions such as love, joy, giving and the feeling of expansion, all of which are positive Piscean emotions. However, if this triad is misused, for example by the action of taking a lover to cover over the fact that a marriage is failing, or by a lack of boundaries, which means that the person is constantly giving to others, it represents negative Pisces and can become just as destructive to the self as negative Scorpio.

LEFT This 15th-century French painting on vellum links the zodiac to the anatomy of man and woman. Each astrological sign rules a part of the body: Aries, head; Taurus, throat; Cancer, chest, and so on downward. Capricorns often have trouble with their knees and Pisceans with their feet.

The Ego and the Self

In Kabbalistic terms, the goal of humanity is to become perfect. Before that can happen, each human being needs to become an individual conscious of his or her own truth, a process known as individuation. This can only take place at the level of Tiferet, which represents the self, and not at the level of Yesod, which represents the ego. The self is who we truly are when all the social and environmental influences are stripped away; the ego is our persona, how we react to situations and how we present ourselves to the world. It is deeply influenced by learned responses from childhood. The self, at Tiferet, is represented by the Sun, and the ego, at Yesod, is represented by the Moon. Thus, to attempt to seek perfection, a person's self needs to be in charge, and the ego should be a reflection of the self.

RIGHT The Sun is the most powerful aspect of the zodiac, as shown in this 18th-century Russian woodcut. It stands over the Moon, which only shines by reflecting the Sun's light. The ego/Moon is incapable of creation or innovation and can only repeat or react to things already in existence.

BELOW The total solar eclipse of 11 August 1999 at the moment of totality. Solar eclipses occur when the Moon passes between the Earth and the Sun. Astrologically, a solar eclipse means that a major change of some kind is likely. Earthquakes often follow solar eclipses.

Astrological or Kabbalistic knowledge can be used to help you understand if your ego is ruling your self and then use the power of free will through discipline to change how you react to life.

UNDERSTANDING THE EGO

If you have ever learned to drive a car, you will remember how tiring it was and how much there was to co-ordinate and remember. Once you had passed your test, slowly but surely, driving became an automatic procedure. At times, it would be hard to remember exactly how you got to a destination as the journey just "happened". This is the purpose of the ego – to run the day-to-day things that do not need the attention of the self.

THE MOON AND THE SUN

In many traditions the Moon is seen as the feminine aspect of the Sun's masculinity. In Kabbalah, both planets are on the middle pillar and are not given overtly gendered characteristics. The Moon reflects the Sun's light but has no light of its own. This shows how the human ego should be a reflection of the self rather than ruling the roost. If the Sun and Moon in a person's chart are in a harmonious aspect to each other, then it is easier for them to use these two aspects of themselves in a manner that will help life to be prosperous and happy. If, however, they are in signs that may conflict with each other – an astrological "square" for example – then the ego and the self may fight for dominance, which leads to a more turbulent and challenging life.

SUN SIGN, MOON SIGN

Many people say that they are nothing like their astrological Sun sign, and this is most likely because they live their life from the Yesodic viewpoint of their Moon sign. Your Moon sign is often more useful to read, as it tells you the likelihood of how your life may be if you do not use free will. From Tiferet upward, there is the possibility of stepping out of the tribal or planetary consciousness and creating your own individual life. As the goal of humanity is individuation, we are all are intended to be more like our Sun sign than our Moon sign. You can calculate your Moon sign by looking in an ephemeris (available in all good book shops) or by finding free astrological software on the Internet.

CONTROLLING THE EGO

Many spiritual traditions speak of eradicating or dissolving the ego, believing that true spirituality is impossible while it still exists. But Kabbalah sees the ego as a vital component in the human psyche – as long as it is understood and developed in order to be the willing servant of the self.

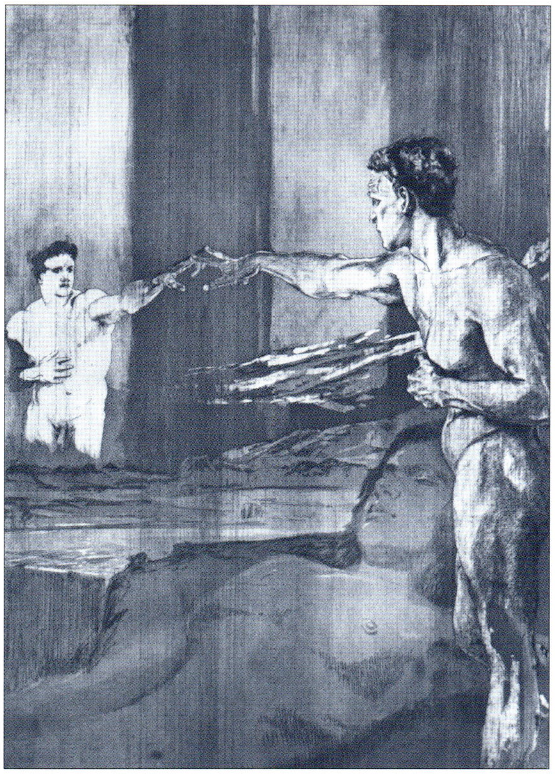

All too often, even in spiritual work, it is the ego that is in charge, which means that the student is deceiving him- or herself about self-development. An ego-led life is a constant series of similar challenges. However, when the self is in charge, the seeker can assess situations consciously and make decisions that are based on the information being given to it from all the Sefirot and triads instead of repeating the same patterns. Then life operates as if the student is rowing a canoe downstream, slightly faster than the river. That way, they can see events coming and avoid them, and stay in charge of the boat's direction. If the ego is in charge, then they travel at exactly the same pace as the river and will be dashed against any rocks or other boats according to the flow of the water and the atmospheric conditions.

Yesod is like fire: a good servant but a bad master. When life appears to repeat patterns – similar destructive relationships, a series of bad bosses or repetitive problems with health – then you can tell that Yesod is over-ruling Tiferet.

ABOVE "An Astrologer Casting a Horoscope", a copy of an illustration from *Utriusque Cosmi Historia* by Robert Fludd. Until the 20th century, birth charts were very rare because few people knew their date of birth. However, event charts were very popular, with the Moon's placement in the zodiac deciding whether or not the question could be answered at that time.

LEFT *Philosopher,* a 19th-century symbolist painting by German Max Klinger. The investigating man reaches for the sky but only finds his own reflection. The ego is a good servant but a bad master. As it is ruled by repetition and habit, it is able to support the self by running the psyche in day-to-day matters. But if it is allowed to overrule our individuality through "shoulds" and "oughts", it prevents any possibility of true happiness.

Numerology and Bible Codes

Kabbalists throughout the centuries have used *gematria* – a system of mathematics that works on a correspondence between the 10 Sefirot and 22 letters of the Hebrew alphabet. The 13th-century Kabbalists believed that the Old Testament was written in this secret code, inspired by God. Today, this is generally known as numerology. Bible codes, which came to prominence in the public domain in 1997, are about a slightly different way of interpreting the Hebrew Bible, through the number of spaces between letters. *Gematria* follows the idea that each letter of an alphabet corresponds to a number. Numerical values of words are added together, and then these words are believed to correspond with other words sharing the same numerical value.

ABOVE Moses and the Israelites crossing the Red Sea, taken from an illuminated Bible text (Exodus 14). The Torah (first five books of the Bible) is filled with symbolism, ranging from psychological archetypes and internal exercises to numerical puzzles.

RIGHT Chaldean conversion tables of Roman and Hebrew letters with their numeric equivalents. Numerology can be used to advise on name changes or fortuitous numbers to look out for when choosing a new home or job.

The first known use of *gematria* was in the 8th century BCE, when the Babylonian king Sargon II built the wall of Khorsabad exactly 16,283 cubits long, because that was the numerical value of his name. It was *gematria* that first suggested the idea of a dove being representative of Jesus in the Christian faith. The Greek word for dove, *peristera*, has the same numerical value as the Greek letters in *alpha* and *omega*, which represent the Beginning and the End from the Book of Revelation.

There are two distinct schools of thought regarding *gematria* within modern Kabbalah. Some approve of its use, while others warn against its practice, saying that it can be a time-consuming distraction.

Calculating Values

Kabbalists are taught that there are four ways to calculate the numerical value of individual letters of the Hebrew alphabet. Absolute value gives the first 10 letters of the Hebrew alphabet numbers from 1 to 10, and all the letters after that are given specific values ranging from 20 to 400. Ordinal value gives each of the 22 a number from 1 to 22. Reduced value gives letters the same value as in Absolute value but then reduces them to the total of their numbers; for example, 20 and 200 are

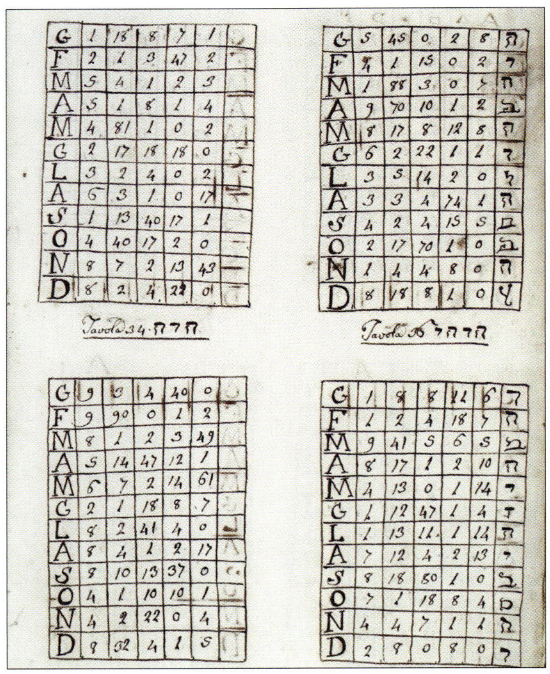

LEFT Nostradamus (Michel de Nostredame) was a 16th-century mystic and prophet who wrote many seemingly outrageous predictions that have influenced the lives of many. Although he is not thought to have practised numerology as the basis of his prophecies, he has been associated with it due to his repeated use of the number four – all his predictions are written in four lines.

reduced to 2, 100 and 10 are reduced to 1. Integral reduced value adds up the numerical value of the letters in a word and adds them together to reduce them to one digit. If the number reduced is more than 10, then it is added together again. For example, a word that totalled 58 letters would be reduced to 13, which would then be reduced to 4. The integral reduced value system is the one most frequently used in modern numerology.

Kabbalists see a relationship between the four different forms of calculation, the four spiritual realms, and the four letters of God's name: YVHV. Much has been made of the fact that the Hebrew letter that represents "W" has a numerical value of six. Therefore, the "www" of the World Wide Web equals the 666 of the Antichrist as revealed in the Book of Revelation.

THE BIBLE CODES

Bible codes, also known as Torah codes, are words, phrases and clusters of words and phrases that some people believe were placed, with intention, within the text of the Bible in order to predict the future. These codes were made famous by the 1997 book *The Bible Code* by Michael Drosnin. They work on a system known as ELS – Equal Distant Letter Sequences – for example, looking for every fourth letter in a certain section of the Bible in order to spell out a predictive sentence. Hotly disputed evidence for the codes was offered in 1994 by three Israelis: Doron Witztum, Eliyahu Rips and Yoav Rosenberg (known as WRR). The men claimed that biographical information about medieval rabbis was encoded in the Hebrew text of Genesis. Events such as the bombing of the Twin Towers in New York are said to have been predicted in the codes. Other predictions included a nuclear war beginning in Jerusalem in 2006, with the participants involved being George W. Bush, Osama Bin Laden and Ariel Sharon; a major earthquake in 2010 and an asteroid hitting Earth in 2012.

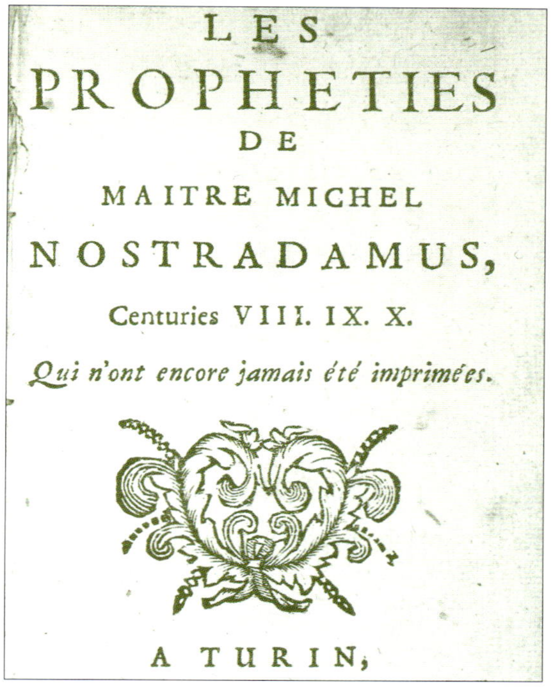

LES
PROPHETIES
DE
MAITRE MICHEL
NOSTRADAMUS,
Centuries VIII. IX. X.
Qui n'ont encore jamais été imprimées.

A TURIN,

LEFT A copy of the 1720 version of the cover of Nostradamus's famous book *Les Propheties*. This work is still regularly published today, and some of the predictions said to have come true include the rise of Napoleon and Hitler – both of whom he referred to as Antichrists. He also predicted a third world war to begin in New York City in 1999.

NOSTRADAMUS

Michel de Nostredame is best known for his book *Les Propheties* (the prophesies), first published in 1555. Nostradamus was a member of a family of Jewish doctors and scholars who had converted to Christianity in 1502, as a result of religious persecution. He studied medicine, herbalism and astrology. Nostradamus' predictions are often confused with Bible codes because they are offered in quatrains, which are simply four-line verses. These are compiled into ten sections called centuries. However, his predictions all came from visions rather than mathematical interpretations of sacred texts.

The Names of God

EVEN THOUGH GOD IS DEPICTED IN KABBALAH AS ABSOLUTE ALL, THERE ARE REFERENCES THROUGHOUT THE TRADITION TO MANY DIFFERENT NAMES, ATTRIBUTED TO ASPECTS OF THE DIVINE. AS WELL AS AYIN, AYIN SOF AND AYIN SOF OR, THERE ARE THE TEN NAMES OF THE SEFIROT OF THE TREE OF LIFE AND FURTHER ASPECTS OF DIVINITY TO BE CONSIDERED. MANY KABBALISTS MEDITATE ON THE NAMES OF GOD, AND SOME SYSTEMS WORK ON COMPLEX NUMEROLOGICAL ASPECTS OF BIBLE PASSAGES, REVEALING A MULTITUDE OF NAMES OF GOD. THERE IS EVEN A 304,805-LETTER NAME OF GOD REVEALED BY RECITING ALL THE LETTERS OF THE TORAH IN A SERIES.

RIGHT A 13th-century painting on vellum showing Old Testament scenes. The ten names of God are used in the Old Testament, but only those initiated into the mysteries were enlightened enough to use the greatest name, and the use of any of the names other than the generic 'The Lord God' was discouraged. According to Kabbalistic teaching, misuse of a name of God may invoke over-severity or lack of justice through karmic law.

The primary name of God is Ehyeh Asher Ehyeh, translated as "I Am That I Am". This is the name that God gave to Moses in the Book of Exodus, and it equates to the Sefira of Keter in the divine world of Azilut. The second name of God is Yahveh, the Wisdom of God, which equates to the Sefira of Hokhmah, with the third name, Elohim, the Understanding of God at Binah. Yahveh is often pronounced "Jehovah".

At Hesed, the name of God is El, the Mercy of God, with Yah, the Judgment of God at Gevurah. At Tiferet, the centre point of the Azilutic Tree of Life, the four names are joined as Yahveh Elohim, translated as the Holy One or the Creator. Below Tiferet, the Sefirot of Nezach and Hod are named Yahveh Zevaot and Elohim Zevaot – the Hosts of Yahveh and Elohim, respectively. Yesod, the Sefira of Foundation, is El Hai Shaddai, The Living Almighty; Malkhut, the Kingdom, is Adonai, Lord, (meaning doorkeeper/superintendent of the household). This aspect of the Divine is also known in Kabbalah as the place of the Messiah, and as Shekhinah, the Daughter of the Voice.

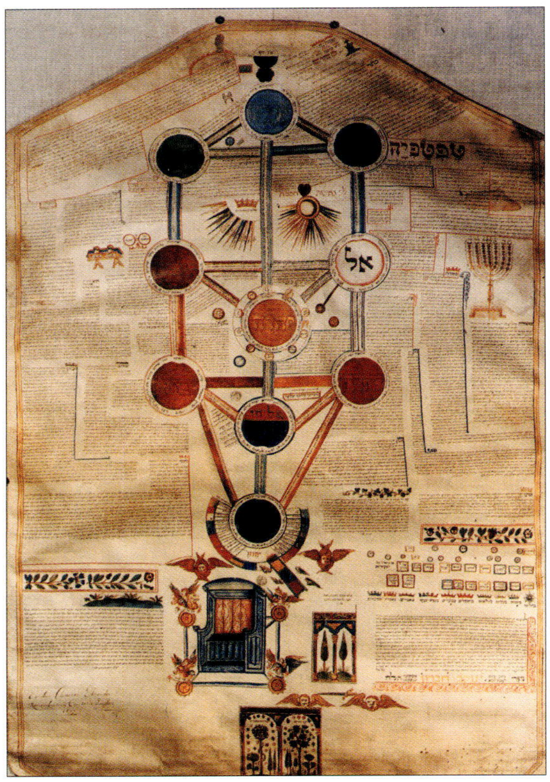

RIGHT A 17th-century Kabbalistic roll with illuminations containing descriptions of the names of God, the Sefirot, the 22 paths that link the Sefirot, and part of the Temple design. Meditation on the names of God has been popular since antiquity, as it is a trusted way to raise human consciousness. However, only the names on the central column should be used if all ten are not to be invoked in one meditation.

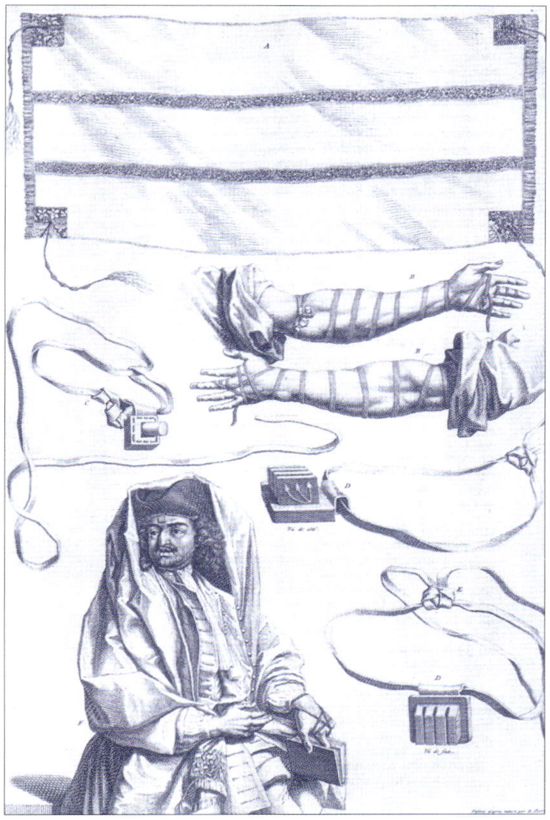

LEFT One of the names of God, Shaddai, is written on scriptural texts contained in tefillin, the two small black boxes that male Orthodox Jews wear on the left arm and forehead for morning prayers every day except for the Sabbath and festivals. The straps attached to the boxes are wound in slightly different ways by Sephardi and Ashkenazi Jews, but the movements correspond to the Sefirot on the Tree of Life. Sacred scripts from Exodus and Deuteronomy are in the black boxes.

NAMES OF GOD IN THE HEBREW BIBLE

Throughout the Hebrew Bible, the names of God are translated as the Lord or the Lord God. In the original Hebrew, however, each of the ten names is used appropriately to demonstrate which aspect of God is active in the stories of the Old Testament. In Genesis, the world and the Divine Man are first described as being created by the Elohim (Divine Idea/ understanding of how the universe is to be). In Genesis 2:7 God creates man a second time by breathing life into dust. But this time, it is Yahveh Elohim who creates, signifying creation at a *different* level. This is man at the spiritual level, one world lower than the Divine Man of Azilut, Adam Kadmon.

"The Lord, my God" is the translation of Yahveh Elohim throughout the Old Testament. God is Yahveh; the Yah aspect of Yahveh is the judgemental part. The two names together balance out. In the books of Job, Daniel and Jonah, God is called El – they are calling on his mercy. In the book of Job, the aspect of God that tests Job is Yahveh and the aspect that Job calls upon for mercy is El. Isaiah alone in the Hebrew Bible calls God "Adonai Yahveh" – The Doorway to Wisdom (or the Christed Wisdom – prophesying the coming of an Anointed One).

JEWISH BELIEFS

It is a belief of Jews that the name of God, commonly known as Jehovah, is more accurately depicted as YHVH. They are not allowed to say the name of God for two reasons. According to legend, it would mean the end of the world. More practical reasons include the belief that to misuse it would have dire consequences – hence the third commandment, "Thou shalt not take the name of the Lord thy God in vain." Also, to use any of the aspects of the names of God would be to create imbalance. Only the Holy One can decide which aspect of himself is appropriate for any circumstance. To refer to the Ineffable as "Lord" using the aspect that was the doorway to the divine was viewed as the safest and best appellation.

In the New Testament, Jesus of Nazareth is known as Kurios (Lord/Master), and God is known as Theos or Kurios Theos (Lord God). This depicts Jesus as an Anointed of God but not as God itself. This vital difference is fundamental to the Kabbalistic reading of the New Testament.

THE 72 NAMES OF GOD

Many Kabbalists use a multitude of different names for God, but the best known are the 72 names. These are, in fact, made up from one 216-letter name of God derived from a sequence of 72 specially-arranged letters found in Exodus 14:19-21, which itself is made up from three verses of 72 letters each. Kabbalists studying *gematria* put together the first letter of verse 14:19, the last letter of verse 14:20 and the first letter of 14:21 to create what is known as a triad. The next triad is created from the second letter of 14:19, the second to last of 14:20 and the second letter of 14:21. This form of *gematria* continues until all the letters are used up.

BELOW Z'ev ben Shimon Halevi's depiction of the Shem ha-Meforash – the ultimate name of God, also known as the Tetragrammaton. It can be written vertically to create the likeness of Adam Kadmon. Every human soul is one cell in this divine being and will be perfect by the end of time.

The Sabbath Eve Service

THE TRADITIONAL JEWISH SABBATH EVE SERVICE, CARRIED OUT IN THE HOME OF ALL ORTHODOX JEWS, FOLLOWS THE KABBALISTIC PRINCIPLE OF BRINGING DIVINITY DOWN TO THE MUNDANE. IT IS A PREPARATION FOR THE SABBATH – THE DAY WHEN NO WORK IS DONE AND WHICH IS DEVOTED INSTEAD TO WORSHIP AND STUDY. THE ORIGINAL TEACHING ABOUT THE SABBATH WAS THAT IT SHOULD BE JOYFUL, NOT RESTRICTIVE, AND A CHANCE TO GET AWAY FROM EVERYDAY TASKS. HOWEVER, THE DEFINITION HAS BECOME BLURRED THROUGH THE CENTURIES. THE IDEA OF A SABBATH HAS BECOME UNPOPULAR IN THE LAST CENTURY. IN JUDAISM, THE SABBATH IS SATURDAY – THE SEVENTH DAY, WHEN GOD RESTED AFTER CREATING THE UNIVERSE. IN CHRISTIANITY IT IS SUNDAY, THE DAY WHEN JESUS WAS RESURRECTED FROM THE DEAD.

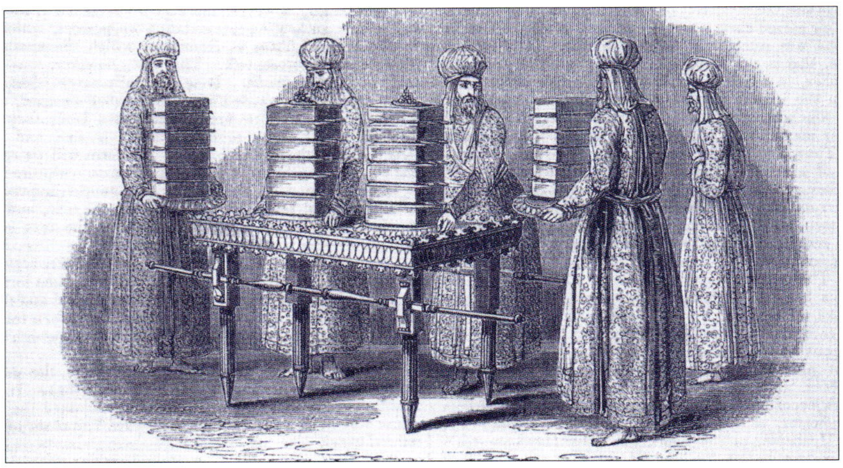

ABOVE Table of Shew-bread – unleavened bread that stood in the sanctuary together with the seven-branched candelabrum and the altar of incense. Every Sabbath, 12 newly baked loaves, representing the 12 tribes of Israel, were put on it in 2 rows, 6 in each, and sprinkled with incense, remaining until the following Sabbath. Then they were replaced by 12 new ones, the incense was burned, and they were eaten by the priests in the holy place, from which they could not be removed.

RIGHT Detail from the Petri Zorni Bible; the lighting of the candles to draw Shekhinah.

As with all Jewish festivals, the Sabbath begins at dusk. However, nowadays, since many Jewish people live further north or south from the equatorial regions and the time of dusk changes through summer and winter, the Sabbath Eve service time has become flexible. In many cases, in the winter, the Sabbath lights are lit at dusk, but the rest of the service is not carried out until the family eats later in the evening. For a Kabbalist, this is not acceptable, as the service is only complete when all four worlds are invoked together.

THE ROLE OF WOMAN AS SHEKHINAH

It is traditionally the senior married woman of the house who lights the Sabbath lights. She recites a prayer of gratitude and hope, and lights two candles to draw Shekhinah, the presence of God, through her, into the home for the duration of the Sabbath. This ritual is so deeply meaningful and powerful when performed consciously that it may explain why Jewish women take no further part in the services that follow. As representatives of the divine, they have no need to perform additional invocations, prayers or rituals but rest, complete in grace. It is from that grace that the masculine draws strength. When a woman is not present, a man will perform the same ceremony, but it is essential for the

THE PURPOSE OF THE SABBATH

The Sabbath creates a time of space and separation when we cease to focus on the mundane and take time for ourselves and our relationship with the Holy One. It is a time to move from Yesodic everyday life to Tiferet, where we can focus on the higher worlds. In ancient times, the only work that was undertaken on the Sabbath was the feeding of livestock. Even picking corn was forbidden (as demonstrated by the Pharisees' criticism of Jesus and his disciples in the Gospel of Matthew 12:2). This was the time when a life of toil could be left behind and replaced by celebration. The principle of the Sabbath was extended to fields – which were rested every seven years – and also to the forgiveness of debts in a seven-year cycle.

ABOVE The priests of the moveable Temple had to wash their hands and feet in the "laver" (a place for washing) before entering the place of the burnt sacrifices and sanctuary. Today, Jews use a ritual bath called a mikvah to cleanse the body and spirit. Among Orthodox Jews, some men – especially in Hasidic circles – use the mikvah regularly, before certain Jewish holidays, before or on the morning of the Sabbath, on Jewish holy days or even daily.

LEFT The clothing of the High Priest of Israel is detailed in Exodus chapter 38. It is coloured gold, blue, purple and red to represent the four worlds, and has a breastplate studded with semi-precious stones representing the 12 tribes of Israel. Shekhinah can be drawn down on the Sabbath Eve without any of these accoutrements.

fulfilment of the ritual for him to focus on the feminine side of his psyche as the receptacle of grace and the wife of God. In theory, single people should attend a Sabbath Eve service with a family, as Shekhinah is said to come to the wife only after her marriage. However, many single Kabbalists perform this ceremony before marriage and even alone, consciously balancing the masculine and feminine energies within themselves.

THE FOUR WORLDS AND THE SABBATH

The Sabbath Eve service draws the light of God down through the four worlds. In a fully Kabbalistic service, the woman will invoke Azilut with the presence of Shekhinah by lighting the candles, and then infuse the wine for the next stage of the service with that presence. Her husband then recites the blessing over the wine, the water and the bread. Wine represents Beriah because of its scent and its transformation through fermentation. The water for the washing of hands represents Yezirah and the cleansing of the psyche, and the bread (which is seasoned with salt) represents the physical world of Asiyyah. After the service is completed, the family or friends gather together to eat a festival meal and salute the Sabbath with the phrase "Shabbat Shalom".

PART FIVE

KABBALAH IN THE MODERN WORLD

Since the 17th century, the influence of Kabbalah has become more obvious through the popularity of hermeticism, alchemy, occultism and magic. It is both the greatest strength and the greatest weakness of an oral tradition that it can be reinterpreted for every age. Today, students have two choices: to work with a system that says the world was created perfect and that evil comes from the misuse of free will, or with one that says the world is imperfect and external evil exists. With the rising popularity of the Kabbalah Centre, the latter system, promoted by the Lurianic tradition, is the far better known. It remains to be seen whether followers of 21st-century Kabbalah are able to work together or if the popularization of forms of the teaching will result in a backlash that returns Kabbalah to the world of secrets.

RIGHT A modern and dynamic interpretation of Kabbalah is depicted in the *Tree of Life* by Albert Herbert. All nations, races and faiths are drawn to the symbolism of the Tree, whether or not there is an inherent knowledge of Kabbalah.

TREE
OF
LIFE

Hasidic Kabbalah

Hasidism or Hasidic Kabbalah, an Ultra-Orthodox Jewish tradition, is a mix of Kabbalah and Rabbinic Judaism. It was developed in the 18th century in Eastern Europe by a Jewish teacher known as the Baal Shem Tov. Like all other forms of Kabbalah (except the Toledano tradition), it is based on Lurianic Kabbalah, but Hasidism teaches that there are sparks of goodness in all things, and everything can be redeemed in order to perfect the world. Despite their emphasis on loving kindness and joy, the Hasidim are the most literally-bound Jewish group, following ancient and 18th-century teachings as the letter of the law. Hasidic Jewish men wear black coats and trousers, white shirts, black hats and have side-locks of curled hair. Their wives shave their heads on marriage and either cover them with a headscarf or wear a wig.

BELOW Hasidic Jews celebrate the Jewish holiday of Purim at a synagogue at Mea Shearim in Jerusalem. Purim is the most joyful of festivals, celebrating the life of Queen Esther, a Jew who saved the lives of her people from a Persian holocaust.

There are 12 major Hasidic groups, the best known of which is the Lubavitch (Russian for "town of brotherly love"). The work of this group's former leader, Rabbi Menachem Mendel Schneerson (1902 –1994) spread Hasidic Judaism widely, particularly in New York. Some groups of the Lubavitch regard him as the Messiah, which has created great controversy throughout the Jewish world.

THE FOUNDING OF HASIDIC KABBALAH

Hasidic Kabbalah was founded by the Baal Shem Tov. Baal Shem means "master of the name", and it is a title given to Kabbalistic leaders who have the ability to contact the higher worlds and supernatural powers. Baal Shem Tov means "master of the good name", a title given to the greatest spiritual leader in the Hasidic Kabbalistic tradition of the 18th century. Such mystics have a great responsibility concerning the development of the teaching in certain epochs or places. In the case of the Baal Shem Tov, it was the healing and rebuilding of a deeply divided and broken Jewish community.

Born Israel ben Eliezer, he was orphaned young and worked as a caretaker in a synagogue in a village in the Ukraine, on the Polish-Russian border. In 1734 he moved to the Ukrainian town of Talust, where he began to be known as a teacher of high repute; one who could make the complex Lurianic Kabbalah accessible even to the simplest Jew. The work of this apparently unlearned man challenged Orthodox Jewish teaching of the time, and he was excommunicated by the Jewish authorities. However, hundreds and then thousands followed his teachings, which became known as Hasidism and spread through Eastern Europe, bringing faith, inspiration and joy to a people torn apart by centuries of war.

The name 'Hasid' comes from Hesed (Loving Kindness), which decribes the focus given to the movement. The Baal Shem Tov was a highly developed soul who could channel the power and purity of Hokhmah (Inspiration) through Hesed to demonstrate that every action, no matter how mundane, could be offered up, in joy, as a redemptive spark to the divine.

The Baal Shem Tov took issue with the Lurianic principle of asceticism and denial; Luria's followers were fond of weeping and lamenting during their prayers, but the Hasidim were encouraged to seek joy in salvation. Even today, the Hasidim are well known for their singing and dancing.

RULES OF KABBALAH

Many groups, such as the Hasidim, believe that following orthodox Biblical traditions, such as immersing the body in the ritual bath, or *mikvah*, and wearing particular clothes, are a vital part of Kabbalistic teaching. This is because customs of Judaism have been applied to Kabbalistic study throughout the centuries, and the tradition has become swathed in complications and secrecy. However, there are no specific rules for Kabbalah other than following the rules of the universe. This means following the structure of the Tree of Life and applying it to the four worlds, with the focus on "helping God to behold God".

ORTHODOX JUDAISM AND KABBALAH

Very few Orthodox Jews would countenance the idea of studying Kabbalah without a deep and proven grounding in Jewish studies, including Hebrew. This viewpoint has both strengths and weaknesses; it ensures that a student of the esoteric has a sound basis on which to work, but it also may tie the student too tightly into the form of Kabbalah. The left-hand pillar of the Tree of Life represents form, while the right-hand pillar represents force. Those who spend all their time studying Hebrew texts and the holy names of God are just as out of balance as those who have a little knowledge and do not apply appropriate boundaries or disciplines to their life and their spiritual learning.

ABOVE The Western, or Wailing, Wall in Jerusalem – the last piece of the Second Temple that still stands. This sacred site is a place of pilgrimage for all Jews, and there is rigid separation of men and women. A prayer placed on a piece of paper in a crack of the wall is said to have particular power.

LEFT A Hasidic Jew reads his prayer book in Safed, Israel. The hair and clothing of the Hasidim date back to the time of the Baal Shem Tov, but despite their importance to members of this group, have no other religious significance. Hasidim always wear a prayer shawl or *tallith* under their clothes, acknowledged as a sacred item in Judaism.

Hermeticism and Alchemy

Hermeticism is a non-Christian tradition of Greek Gnosticism based on 15 tracts known as the *Corpus Hermeticum*. These came to prominence in the Renaissance court of Cosimo de Medici in the 15th century, but date back to classical Greek times. Hermeticism is included in the modern Kabbalah section due to its relevance to the development of inter-faith studies in the 19th to 21st centuries and its importance to ritual magicians, alchemists, Kabbalists and Masons. In the 19th century, London was one of the occult centres of the world and home to Madame Blavatsky, founder of the Theosophical Society, a group devoted to encouraging the study of comparative religion, philosophy and science, and strongly influenced by hermeticism.

RIGHT Helena Petrovna Blavatsky (1831–1891), the Russian-born theosophist who helped found the Theosophical Society with Henry Steel Olcott in 1875. Madame Blavatsky claimed to possess psychic powers, and despite being discredited by the Society for Psychical Research, maintained a loyal following.

HERMES TRISMEGISTUS

Hermeticism is named after Hermes Trismegistus (Hermes the three times great) – an amalgam of the Egyptian god Thoth and the Greek god Hermes, also known as Mercury. Allegedly, Hermes is the author of dozens of mystical tractates, including the *Corpus Hermeticum* and the perhaps better-known *Emerald Tablet*. It is generally believed that these texts were channelled and that the books themselves were written by anonymous scribes. The text of the *Emerald Tablet* totals just 13 lines – but it is the cornerstone of the hermetic movement's foundational belief of "as above, so below".

RIGHT A 17th-century depiction of the secret process of the perfecting of the Philosopher's Stone. In the view of spiritual alchemy, making such a stone would bring enlightenment upon the maker. The crowned monster is a symbol of the *materia prima*, the first matter. The triple crown symbolizes the three kingdoms in outer nature (animal, vegetable, mineral), the three principles within man (salt, mercury, sulphur), and the alchemical terms for thinking, feeling and willing.

The basic premise of all hermeticism is "as above, so below", the idea that the structure of heaven and Earth are the same and that discord or harmony in each affects the other. Therefore, all human action and thought has an effect on the higher worlds. This is very similar to the Kabbalistic idea of human actions and thoughts permeating the four worlds.

Most occult seekers have studied hermeticism, and it was especially important to the Hermetic Order of the Golden Dawn. The hermetic teaching of "ascended masters" became very popular for New Age seekers in the late 20th century.

The origin of the text and why it is known as the *Emerald Tablet* are both unknown, but its text reveals its authorship thus: "Therefore am I called Hermes Trismegistus, having the three parts of the philosophy of the whole world." This work languished in relative obscurity until the Middle Ages, when it began to circulate throughout the alchemical community through contact with Muslim mystics. Scholars believe the original was written in Greek, but the oldest surviving copies are Arabic translations.

KABBALAH AND ALCHEMY

Alchemy dates back to ancient Egypt and is also known from Mesopotamia, Persia, India and China. There are many alchemical schools, but Western alchemy has always been closely associated with Hermeticism and followed the belief in four basic elements – earth, water, air and fire – also represented in the Kabbalistic four worlds.

Following on from the hermetical belief of "as above, so below", alchemists attempt to work on all levels, including the idea of transforming physical matter in the belief that understanding this will help them comprehend the higher worlds. In alchemy, the intention is to create gold from base metal – and many of the amalgams and metals that we use today have come from ancient alchemists' experiments. Gunpowder, leather tanning, ceramics and glass manufacture all benefited from the work of ancient alchemists. The Philosopher's Stone is a mythical substance that was also sought – it was believed to heal sickness, prolong life and give inspiration.

To spiritual seekers, however, including Kabbalists, alchemy is not intended to be the art of creating physical gold – but of melding psychological gold from the base metal of the psyche. Gold represents Tiferet, so it is the alchemy of finding harmony among all the Sefirot that leads us to the position where we have access to the spiritual world, and from there to divinity. Alchemical symbols and motifs are complex, and the practice of any kind of alchemy requires discipline and *kavanah* (good intention), as this spiritual science can be extremely dangerous to the uninitiated.

LEFT Alchemy espouses the belief that each of the elements permeates the others. This image, *Mutus Liber* (Silent Book) shows the benign light of a higher world spreading down to Earth past the Sun and Moon. Below, the Greek god Mercury, with a winged cap, assists the masculine and feminine aspects of humanity with the transformation of earthly matter.

LEFT The idea of alchemy appears to have been born almost simultaneously in ancient Egypt, India and China as a study of how matter is made up of the four elements of nature – fire, earth, air and water. It was named *khemia*, the Greek word for Egypt, and when Egypt was occupied by the Arabs in the 7th century, '*al*-' was added to the word *khemia*.

Kabbalah and Occultism

Kabbalah has been used as the basis for many occult traditions. Probably the most famous of the world's occult orders – and for many years the public face of Kabbalah – was the Hermetic Order of the Golden Dawn, founded in London in 1888 by three Freemasons, Dr W. R. Woodman, Dr W. W. Westcott and S. L. MacGregor Mathers. They were interested in Rosicrucianism, an occult fraternity based in Germany. Kabbalah – or, as they spelled it, Qabalah – trained its members in what the group called "high magic", meditation, concentration, ritual and evocation (the art of calling forth spirits, angels and demons). This was both to learn about the inner world and to attempt to control the external world.

BELOW The Rosicrucian symbol of the Golden Dawn, using the Jewish Star of David and the astrological signs for Sun and Moon. The dark and light of the yin-yang symbol of masculine and feminine principles is also prominent.

BELOW RIGHT Aleister Crowley, a man who revelled in notoriety, sexual excess and magical practices. His own lack of self-discipline led to his downfall, as he was unable to stop Yesod from ruling his psyche.

The Golden Dawn developed a complex system of interpretation of the paths of the Tree of Life, based largely on the Sefer Yezirah. Two of the most famous members of this group were Dion Fortune and Aleister Crowley.

Dion Fortune

One of the best-known occultists of the 20th century, Dion Fortune, was born Violet Mary Firth in 1890. She adopted the family motto "Deo, non Fortuna" (by God, not by Chance) as her name as she became more interested in mysticism. Fortune believed that she had been a temple priestess in Atlantis in a past life. She became a member of a fringe order of the Hermetic Order of the Golden Dawn, known as the London Temple of the Alpha and Omega Lodge of the Stella Matutina. Later, in 1919, she formed her own order, known as the Fraternity of the Inner Light, based upon esoteric and Kabbalistic Christianity but strongly influenced by Jungian psychology. Fortune moved to Glastonbury, where she claimed to be in spiritual contact with the Greek philosopher Socrates and the Arthurian wizard Merlin. She founded the Chalice Orchard Club in Glastonbury and the Belfry, a London

temple dedicated to the mysteries of the Egyptian goddess Isis. Her books included *Glastonbury: Avalon of the Heart* and *Psychic Self-Defence*, and she still has a large following. Dion Fortune died of leukaemia in 1946 at the age of 54.

ALEISTER CROWLEY

A controversial figure in the Golden Dawn and spin-off groups that followed it was Aleister Crowley, who called himself "the Beast". A writer, poet, and occultist, he is now firmly established as a folk antihero. The British press described him as "the wickedest man in the world", and his most famous saying is "do what thou wilt shall be the whole of the law." Crowley emphasized the magical (which he spelled "magickal") tradition, drawing power from nature and expecting the natural world to be obedient to his will. He travelled widely, seeking knowledge, and settled for a number of years in Sicily with a group of disciples at the Abbey of Thelema. Stories of drugs, orgies, and magical ceremonies led to his expulsion from Italy. His promiscuity with women and men is said to have inspired the "free-love" generation of the 1960s, but he died doubting his own philosophies, a penniless drug addict. It was mostly through Crowley's work and that of his former secretary, Israel Regardie, that Golden Dawn teachings were revealed to the world. Regardie was a prolific writer, and two of his books, *The Tree of Life* and *A Garden of Pomegranates*, both written while he was in his early 20s, became classics of the genre.

THE ROSICRUCIANS

Rosicrucianism surfaced in 1614, in Germany, when a manuscript called *Fama Fraternitatis: The Declaration of the Worthy Order of the Rosy Cross* was published. It told of the life and work of Christian Rosenkreutz who, it alleged, had lived more than a century earlier. Two more documents, *The Confession Fraternitatis* and *The Chymical Wedding of Christian Rosenkreutz*, were also published, although no trace of the man or his followers was ever found. Rosicrucianism is based largely on Egyptian alchemy, Kabbalah, the principle of inner knowledge and the belief in reincarnation. Much of the writing in the documents is Kabbalistic, and it also bears a strong resemblance to the work of Dr John Dee, the famous mystic of Queen Elizabeth I's court.

LEFT The Knight of Cups card from the Thoth Tarot deck designed for Aleister Crowley by Frieda Harris. Apart from his mother, Frieda Harris was probably the longest-lasting most platonic relationship in Crowley's life, and she frequently helped him financially.

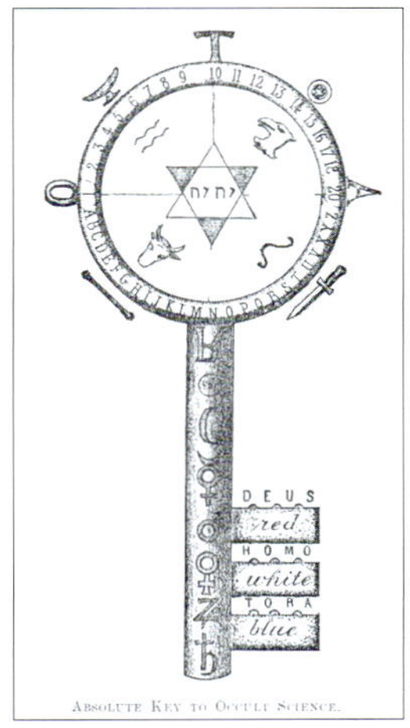

ABOVE The cover image of *The Absolute Key to Occult Science – The Tarot of the Bohemians* by Papus. This was subtitled *The Most Ancient Book in the World, for the Exclusive Use of Initiates*. It's a complex book detailing correspondences between tarot, the Tetragrammaton, numerology and astrology.

LEFT The Tree of Life is believed to be one of the sources for the game of Snakes and Ladders, with the serpent of the Garden of Eden lying in wait for the spiritual aspirant as they attempt to climb to higher worlds. The game of hopscotch is also believed to originate with the Tree. This image is from the private notebook of a Rosicrucian in the 1920s.

KABBALAH AND THE TAROT

THE TAROT IS A DECK OF CARDS CONTAINING ESOTERIC IMAGES USED FOR DIVINATION AND SELF-DISCOVERY. A TAROT DECK HAS 78 CARDS, 22 OF WHICH ARE TRUMP CARDS, RELATING TO THE 22 LETTERS OF THE HEBREW ALPHABET, COLLECTIVELY CALLED THE MAJOR ARCANA. THE TAROT APPEARS TO HAVE ORIGINATED IN 14TH-CENTURY ITALY, ALTHOUGH THERE ARE COMPARABLE (BUT MUCH MORE ANCIENT) CHINESE AND INDIAN SYSTEMS. IT WAS THE 19TH-CENTURY FRENCH OCCULTIST ELIPHAS LEVI WHO MADE THE FIRST LINK BETWEEN THE TAROT AND KABBALAH. THIS WAS COMPLEMENTED, NEAR THE END OF THE 19TH CENTURY, BY THE WORK OF GOLDEN DAWN MEMBERS S. L. MACGREGOR MATHERS AND A. E. WAITE, WHO CONCLUDED THAT THE CONNECTION WITH KABBALAH WORKED FOR THE WHOLE PACK, NOT JUST THE TRUMP SUIT.

RIGHT Eliphas Levi was born Alphonse Louis Constant in 1810. He trained as a priest but preferred the occult. He taught that animal magnetism was an energy controlled by the devil and that a magician's willpower was limitless. Aleister Crowley, who was born the same year that Levi died, claimed to be his reincarnation.

THE MAJOR ARCANA

This section of the deck comprises 22 picture cards, which are numbered and have Hebrew names given to them. Each describes a condition or a set of laws at work, but different readers of tarot may give different interpretations to each according to their own particular belief system and psychological development. The 22 major tarot cards are often aligned with the 22 paths on the Tree of Life – but there are several different interpretations of which card goes where. The path between Nezach and Tiferet, for example, is variously ascribed to Death, the Hanged Man and the Star, whereas the paths

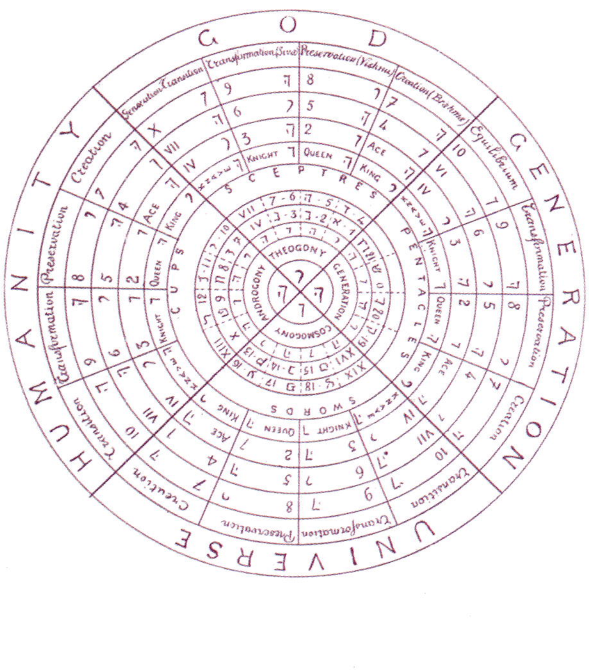

RIGHT A page from *The Absolute Key to Occult Science – The Tarot of the Bohemians*, by Gerard Encausse, a Spanish-born French physician, hypnotist, and popularizer of occultism. Encausse's pseudonym, "Papus", was taken from Eliphas Levi's *Nuctemeron of Apollonius of Tyana* and means "physician". Papus is primarily remembered as an author of books on magic, Kabbalah and the tarot, and as a prominent figure in occultist organizations and Parisian spiritualist and literary circles of the late 19th and early 20th centuries.

This century has seen further interpretation of exactly how the tarot deck fits on to the Tree of Life. Although the best-known tarot deck is still the Rider-Waite tarot, there are now tarot packs as diverse as the angel tarot, shining tribe tarot and Thoth tarot. Many of the new designs leave only a basic idea of what the original tarot images might have been, but the powerful symbolism remains.

between Keter and Binah, and Keter and Hokhmah are ascribed to the Fool, the Juggler, the Empress and the Emperor. Basic inconsistencies can be spotted easily, such as the Empress being placed on the right-hand (masculine) side of the Tree of Life.

THE FOUR SUITS

The minor pack is composed of four suits, each made up from ten numbers beginning with the ace. The four suits can easily be identified as the four worlds, with Wands (clubs) representing Azilut, Swords (spades) representing Beriah, Cups (hearts) corresponding to Yezirah, and Pentacles (diamonds) representing Asiyyah. Each court card also represents a level: all the Kings represent Azilut; all the Queens, Beriah; the Knights, Yezirah; and the Pages, Asiyyah. Therefore, the Queen of Wands represents the Beriatic level in Azilut and the Knight of Swords represents the Yeziratic level in Beriah.

The ten numbered cards are each assigned to one of the ten Sefirot, with the ace as Keter, the two as Hokhmah, the three as Binah, the four as Hesed, the five as Gevurah and so on. Therefore, the six of Pentacles represents the Tiferet of the Asiyyatic world, and the six of Cups represents the Tiferet of the Yeziratic world. Interpreting them in such a way is helpful in a tarot reading.

THE PATHS

Pathwork on the Tree of Life is for the advanced student only, and it can be beset with illusions. It is generally perceived that each Sefira represents an attribute of a student's psyche, and therefore the path between particular Sefirot represents that person's personal journey between the attributes. For example, the path between Hod and Gevurah would represent how well (or badly) an individual person could use discrimination to filter the information that they might have read or heard. There is no single interpretation available of each path, and most modern Kabbalists are taught that they can only begin to comprehend the meanings of the paths once they have, first, fully understood the Sefirot, the triads and the four worlds.

ABOVE The Sun, the Wheel of Fortune, the Lovers and the Fool from the Rider-Waite tarot pack, which originated within the Golden Dawn. This is still the definitive modern tarot used by countless practitioners. According to legend, when religious persecution stops the dissemination of mystical knowledge, it is preserved in games and children's stories. Both playing cards and the game of Snakes and Ladders are based on Kabbalistic principles.

TAROT AND RELIGION

There is a legend, dating back to 1778, that tells of a soldier seeing the spiritual significance of each of the cards in a deck and using them as an aid to prayer and meditation. This is always associated with the Christian faith through the song *Deck of Cards*, sometimes known as *A Soldier's Prayer Book*, which was written in 1948 by T. Texas Tyler and recorded by (among others) Tex Ritter in 1948 and Wink Martindale in 1959. Both the tarot deck and the mundane card deck are unique in that they can represent the religious symbology of all faiths. They all lead to the concept of One and tell of the trials and joys of the paths to wholeness.

Kabbalah and Magic

For Kabbalists, the Tree of Life diagram is the "image" of God in which the Bible tells us that mankind is made. Knowledge of the psychological world of Yezirah can mean understanding God – and that can confer psychological power on a student of this mystery tradition. It means that he or she can see the strengths and weaknesses of another human being through psychic means, and this could be used as a form of manipulation, which is the basis of magic. For people in the modern world, magic is either "white" or "black". Many white witches now run advice columns in women's magazines, and there is a blending of the concepts of spirituality and magic. The modern confusion about what magic actually is has become a major concern within the orthodox religious world.

RIGHT Moses changing a staff into a serpent before the Egyptian pharoah. Moses' trick was easily emulated by Egyptian magicians until he focused on God. Then his magic was able to overcome that of the Egyptians.

BELOW "The Triumph of Venus, the Month of April", with its zodiac sign of Taurus, in a 15th-century Italian fresco. Both magic and astrology belong to the Yeziratic realm and can be overruled by the use of free will and spiritual knowledge.

Humanity has learned, particularly in the 20th century onward, that it will feel happier if it controls the world around it. However, this takes great energy and effort and blinds us to the spiritual workings of the world. To invoke what humanity believes is the correct outcome is, all too frequently, to misinterpret the Divine Plan.

YEZIRAH AND MAGIC

To a Kabbalist, magic, like astrology, exists only in the world of Yezirah. Magic is defined as bending the Yeziratic world for someone's own will – whether it be for good or for bad. Yezirah is manipulated by any invocation or prayer demanding a specific result, such as asking for a girl you like to fall in love with you. It is an infringement on the other person's free will to cast a spell or call for supernatural aid to make someone act in a way that they do not intend. At its most basic level, modern advertising is a form of magic – especially the repetition of words and phrases and the implication that certain products and ideas will make people stronger, fitter and more loveable.

Good or "white" magic, which has become increasingly popular in the modern world, is still an effort to bend the "matrix" of the Yeziratic world. Examples would be to pray or cast a spell for a specific person to win a competition, or to do an incantation for someone to recover from sickness.

WARNINGS AGAINST MAGIC

All forms of magic are deemed unwise and even dangerous by orthodox and modern Kabbalists. While they believe it is perfectly possible for a human being to impose his or her will on a person or situation through magical means, the performing of any magic (with the obvious exception of conjuring tricks) pushes the matrix of the universe out of balance. It takes a continual effort of will to keep the magic working, so sooner or later the pressure of the universe to return to its correct form will cause the magic to rebound on its creator.

Sir Isaac Newton's Third Law of Motion explains the process: "For every action there is an equal and opposite reaction." If healing or prayer is sent to someone, the equivalent healing or prayer returns. If magical manipulation is sent to someone, then the equivalent magic returns.

All the major religions of the world also warn against magic. The original idea behind the warnings was that magic can be incredibly harmful to its perpetrator. The Book of Exodus tells how the magicians of the pharaoh could not out-challenge Moses, who had divine power. Harsh terms are applied for those who reject the word of God and impose the word of man, as is demonstrated by the prophet Samuel's words to King Saul in Samuel 15:23: "For rebellion is as the sin of witchcraft, and stubbornness is as iniquity and idolatry. Because thou hast rejected the word of the Lord, He hath also rejected thee from being king."

ABOVE Heinrich Cornelius Agrippa (1486–1535) was a German magician, alchemist and Kabbalist who wrote influential Renaissance esoterica. His three-volume *De Occulta Philosophia* was written when he was just 23 but not published for another 20 years. Agrippa's works were read by the young Victor Frankenstein in Mary Shelly's *Frankenstein*.

SPIRITUAL WORK AND MAGIC

There is a clear difference between spiritual work – invoking the aid of the divine – and thinking one knows better than God. Some people who say they practise as witches are working with prayer to invoke "the highest good" for clients who ask for help. This is not, technically, magic at all. To invoke God's will or the "highest" good for someone is to move beyond the world of Yezirah to the spiritual world of Beriah. Likewise, to offer "healing" is not magical, because it also asks for a perfect outcome (many healers' work involves helping people to die in peace). The challenge with esoteric practices being available in the public domain is that the spiritual beginner often cannot grasp the vital differences between the levels with which they are working.

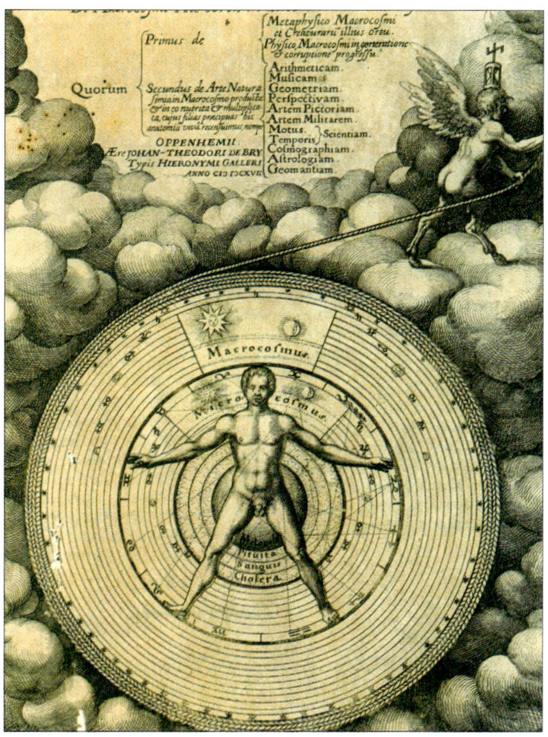

LEFT An engraving by Robert Fludd, from *Utriusque Cosmi Historia*, showing a detail of man as a microcosm of the universe, or macrocosm, with four humours (sanguine, phlegmatic, choleric, melancholic). Self-knowledge is powerful magic that can transform lives. This magic focuses on understanding the inner levels rather than trying to alter outside circumstances. However, understanding other people's psyches can tempt us to manipulate them.

TOLEDANO KABBALAH

TOLEDANO KABBALAH, ALSO CALLED THE WORK OF UNIFICATION, BECAME KNOWN IN THE WESTERN WORLD IN THE 1970S. ITS GOAL IS TO RECREATE THE ESSENCE OF THE GOLDEN AGE OF SPAIN, WHEN CHRISTIAN, MUSLIM AND JEW LIVED TOGETHER IN HARMONY. THIS TRADITION IS UNIQUE IN THAT IT FOCUSES ON PRE-LURIANIC KABBALAH – CITING THE GENESIS TEXT "AND GOD SAW THAT IT WAS VERY GOOD" AS A REFUTAL OF ISAAC LURIA'S THEORY THAT THE VESSELS OF CREATION SHATTERED. TOLEDANO KABBALAH IS OF PARTICULAR INTEREST FOR PEOPLE WISHING TO STUDY KABBALISTIC KNOWLEDGE FROM THE TIME OF JESUS OF NAZARETH OR ANY OTHER GREAT TEACHERS WHO LIVED BEFORE THE 16TH CENTURY. IT IS NOW TAUGHT WORLDWIDE AND IS KNOWN FOR ITS CLARITY OF INTERPRETATION FOR THE MODERN AGE.

RIGHT An 18th-century Italian illuminated scroll of the biblical Book of Esther. This has always been a controversial book, as it is the only one in the Old Testament that does not mention God. Esther is written in ten chapters and chronicles the outer story of the attempted genocide of the Jews in Persia together with the inner story of Esther's psychological development from pauper to queen and saviour of her people.

This form of Kabbalah is called "Toledano" because the Spanish city of Toledo was the centre of the post-Golden-Age time of scholarship and mysticism in the 11th century. Mystics and scholars from all three of the "People of the Book" – Jews, Christians and Muslims – came to Toledo to study and work together at this time.

BACK TO BASICS

Toledano Kabbalists work in a School of the Soul rather than as individuals. A School of the Soul is a group of people with the same spiritual interests at heart who teach and learn together. Such a school will last for 50–100 years before its original impulse dies and a new school takes its place. Those who participate in this tradition meet in groups to discuss the work and to understand the processes of their own souls, the souls of nations, the history of the world and the Divine Plan. Their path is essentially practical; the understanding of how Kabbalah can aid life in the everyday world.

Although the revitalized tradition was founded by a Jewish man, Z'ev ben Shimon Halevi, and honours Jewish tradition, there are Toledano Kabbalists worldwide, from many differing faiths. The Japanese branch of the school, for example, is working to equate the Kabbalistic Tree of Life and Jacob's Ladder with the Shinto faith. The school does not work with *gematria* or meditations on the

RIGHT Queen Esther, who according to the Toledano tradition was the first known female Messiah or Anointed of God. Esther's story is celebrated in the Jewish festival of Purim. Her son, Darius, was responsible for freeing the Jews from years of captivity in Persia. The only other woman to have a book in the Bible named after her is Ruth.

name of God, rather it focuses on a very deep level of understanding of the Tree of Life and Jacob's Ladder, together with disciplined group contemplative meditation similar to the Merkabah chariot-riding of the 1st century.

Z'EV BEN SHIMON HALEVI

Warren Kenton is a Sephardi Jew who lives in London, whose books are written under his Hebrew name, Z'ev ben Shimon Halevi. He is the author of 14 books on Kabbalah, including a novel about the life of a messianic Jewish figure at the time of the Spanish Inquisition, *The Anointed*.

Halevi's specific teaching is in revealing and updating the Kabbalah of the Golden Age, and his work specifies that there is always a Messiah alive in every generation; this individual is known as the Axis of the Age. Most of them have been hidden, although some – perhaps such as Jesus, the Buddha, Ghandi or Queen Esther (the Old Testament Queen of Persia who saved the Jews from a holocaust) – came to prominence because their time and purpose required it. Together with these great men and women, there are a number of Tzadikim, or wise people, who help lift the spiritual energy of the world through living a good life and spiritual consciousness.

WOMEN IN THE TOLEDANO TRADITION

The Toledano tradition has many female teachers, subscribing to the view that the rebbitzen (the rabbi's wife) would teach women at the *mikvahs* in ancient days. The *mikvah* is the single-sex sacred bath where men and women in Orthodox Judaism go for ritual cleansing. This is required after contact with the sick or the dead or, for a woman, seven days after the end of menstruation. Ritual separation between the sexes is upheld for the duration of a woman's period, and in ancient days this time was seen as sacred. At this time, if at no other, the women relied on the rebbitzen for their teaching. She, therefore, would need to have a deep knowledge of the spirituality of women as well as of the Torah. Toledano Kabbalists are not Orthodox Jews and do not practise ritual separation nor use the *mikvah,* and in this tradition women teach both sexes, as do men.

THE WORK OF UNIFICATION

According to Halevi's books, the primary work for the Toledano Kabbalah school is to integrate learning among Jews, Christians and Muslims. The adherents of these great religions are known as the "People of the Book" because all three religions were founded on the Old Testament of the Bible. Although the Kabbalistic teaching of this tradition is primarily Jewish, it acknowledges great teachers such as the Buddha, Muhammad and Jesus as being Tzadikim – wise ones at the level of being God's Anointed (placed at the Malkhut of Azilut).

LEFT Z'ev Ben Shimon Halevi's depiction of the task that underlies the personal development work of the Kabbalist: to seek to join that which is above to that which is below. Here, he becomes conscious of the two higher worlds and draws the divine light down through the world of Formation, with its symbolic planetary archetypes arranged in a Sefirotic tree, into himself and so to earth.

BELOW A set of stairs leading to a *mikvah*, or sacred bath, in the ruins of the ancient Essene settlement of Qumran, in Israel. Fragments of the Dead Sea Scrolls have been found there since 1947.

THE KABBALAH CENTRE

THE KABBALAH CENTRE IS A HIGHLY SUCCESSFUL INTERNATIONAL ORGANIZATION DEVOTED TO THE TEACHING OF UNIVERSALIZED KABBALISTIC PRINCIPLES. FOUNDED IN 1969 BY THE CONTROVERSIAL PHILIP BERG, THE KABBALAH CENTRE NOW HAS MORE THAN 50 BRANCHES WORLDWIDE, INCLUDING MULTIMILLION-DOLLAR HEADQUARTERS IN LOS ANGELES, TEL AVIV, LONDON, NEW YORK AND TORONTO. IT HAS DONE MORE TO BRING KABBALAH TO THE NOTICE OF THE WORLD THAN ANY OTHER GROUP. IT IS A PUBLISHER OF BOOKS IN MORE THAN TEN LANGUAGES, WHICH SELL IN THEIR MILLIONS. THE KABBALAH CENTRE EMPIRE NOW INCLUDES LEARNING BRANCHES AROUND THE WORLD, A CHARITABLE FOUNDATION, A CHILDREN'S EDUCATION PROGRAMME AND A PUBLISHING EMPIRE. HOWEVER, RUMOUR AND SPECULATION SURROUND THE CENTRE, AND IT HAS FACED MANY ACCUSATIONS OF BEING A CULT.

BELOW "The Rav", Philip Berg, founder of the worldwide movement that is the Kabbalah Centre. The Rav is a controversial figure as is common with charismatic leaders. He is now very rarely seen in public, and his sons have taken over his work.

The Kabbalah Centre venerates the teaching of Isaac Luria but develops his theme of the shattering of the Sefirot. Their modern version of the teaching says that the Holy One created the vessels (Sefirot) in order to have something to receive the light that he wished to flow. However, the Sefirot did not wish only to receive, but also to give, and resisted the light. The Holy One then withdrew the light and, when the Sefirot mourned its loss, re-flowed it. At that point, the Sefirot shattered, being unable to handle the light.

The task of humanity, in order to repair the vessels, is to learn to receive the light for the sole purpose of sharing it. The idea of receiving only for one's self or giving only when one's self is full to overflowing, is taught to be the cause of the world's troubles today. The centre works mainly with interpretations from the Zohar and also meditations on the holy Hebrew letters, claiming that reading or speaking the names creates a deep resonance within the reader, and that it is not necessary to understand them. Students are not taught about the Tree of Life or the principles of the four worlds.

THE BERGS

Philip Berg was born Feivel Gruberger in Brooklyn, New York. He married the niece of a well-known Kabbalist, Rabbi Brandwein, and distributed his books in the USA. Berg, also known as "the Rav", claims that he was ordained in the USA early in the 1950s, and received an additional ordination in Israel from Rabbi Brandwein. This has not been confirmed by Rabbi Brandwein's close associates.

According to an article by Aynat Fishbein in the Israeli magazine *Tel Aviv,* published in 1994, Berg's claim that he continues in the path of his own teachers, Kabbalistic Rabbi Ashlag and Rabbi

Brandwein, and that they are the original founders of his centre, has been soundly refuted both by Rabbi Ashlag's grandson and by Rabbi Brandwein's associate Baruch Horenchik.

In the early 1970s, Berg married his second wife, Karen, and it is their sons, Yehuda and Michael, who lead the teaching today. However, Berg is often pilloried in the press for having left his first wife Rizka and their eight children for Karen. This is not mentioned in his official autobiography – but it is not an uncommon occurrence in the modern world. Much is also made of the fact that he began life with the name Feivel Gruberger and was an insurance salesman. Berg and his sons are also accused of using New Age ghostwriters to help them write books that are accessible and attractive. However, this is not unusual in the world of celebrity publishing.

IS IT A CULT?

As with many spiritual groups, the Kabbalah Centre has often been accused of being a cult. The Internet is filled with horror stories from ex-members claiming that the centre extorted thousands of dollars from them in return for a cure for illness; that students at the centres are used as "slave-labour"; and that relationships and marriages have been broken up because the partner was not willing to join. Others have spoken of feeling threatened when they wanted to leave or had not given money, having been told that they were under attack by satanic forces. The Kabbalah Centre is featured in more than 100 articles on a website devoted to cults, www.nickross.com, hosted by the Nick A. Ross Institute for the study of Destructive Cults, Controversial Groups and Movements. This carries stories of the arrest of a prominent member of one of the Kabbalah Centre's headquarters for fraud after promising a cure for cancer, tales of coercion and threats. None of these accusations, to date, have been substantiated.

ABOVE The Kabbalah Centre in Los Angeles includes a fully-functioning school that takes pupils from nursery school to graduation. It is currently expanding and is to replace its existing facilities (pictured) with a new 38,240ft^2 four-storey building with up to 20 classrooms.

FAR LEFT Madonna (left) taking part in a Kabbalah conference in Tel Aviv, Israel, in 2004, with some 2,000 participants from 22 countries. Madonna and her husband, Guy Ritchie, attended a lecture given by her Los Angeles Kabbalah teacher, Eitan Yardeni.

LEFT Yehuda Berg, co-director of the Kabbalah Centre and son of "the Rav", holds up a copy of his *Red String Book*. The Kabbalah Centre has an outstanding media and PR wing that enables its work to be promoted throughout the world.

Claims and Celebrities

One of the reasons for the success of the Kabbalah Centre is that it has attracted attention from many non-Jewish celebrities, including Madonna and Britney Spears. However, some of the claims made by Madonna and practices such as wearing a red string bracelet have sparked controversy. Financial practices at the Centre have also raised concern, as members are expected to donate money regularly (a system similar to the Old Testament practice of tithing). The Centre has a thriving retail trade, including books, CDs, jewellery, "Kabbalah cures", creams and make-up, astrological charts, baby accessories – most carrying at least one of the 72 names of God – and the famous red string bracelets, as well as events, pilgrimages and workshops.

ABOVE Roseanne Barr discusses her new reality series, *The Real Roseanne Show*, with television critics during an ABC television network presentation.

RIGHT Madonna at a reading of one of her children's books in Los Angeles. She has denied claims that she dedicated her album *Confessions on a Dance Floor* to Rabbi Isaac Luria, saying that the song "Isaac" is named after her co-singer on the track, Yitzhak (Isaac) Sinwani.

American superstar Madonna is a keen member of the Kabbalah Centre and is its greatest advocate. She is the author of a Kabbalistic children's book, *The English Roses,* in which the heroine is named Binah, after the Sefira of Understanding. Madonna has adopted a Hebrew name – that of the Biblical heroine Esther – and wears a red thread on her wrist to ward off the "evil eye". This is an ancient folkloric belief that a person can be harmed by the energy emitted when other people envy their good luck or success in life. There is no doubt that Madonna's fame has helped the Kabbalah Centre, whether or not it has been through inspiring others or creating controversy. In 2004, she caused an uproar after claiming at a press conference that she considered herself the "Messiah of Kabbalah". Madonna has been quoted in the *New York Daily News* and the *London Evening Standard* as saying that she would be less controversial if she had joined the Nazi Party rather than the Kabbalah Centre.

RED STRING

To wear something red is part of ancient Jewish folklore rather than Kabbalistic lore. It is said to protect the wearer from the "evil eye". Nowadays it is sold by the Kabbalah Centre to protect against the power of envy. The sacred red string has been wrapped around the Jewish Matriarch Rachel's tomb, which is located on the Southern West Bank, outside Jerusalem, and is considered the third holiest site in Judaism after the Temple Mount and the Cave of the Machpelah on the West Bank (believed to contain the graves of Adam and Eve, Abraham and Sarah, Isaac and Rebekah, and Jacob and Leah).

Rachel's story in the book of *Genesis* does not suggest her as a strong protective icon. She was tricked by her sister Leah and had to share her husband with her sister. She was barren for years, dabbled in magic, stole some idols from her father and died in childbirth. However, in Matthew 2:18, Rachel weeps for her children, which is seen as the soul of the matriarch overseeing the welfare of her descendents. The red string bracelets associated with Rachel cost approximately £18.

KABBALAH WATER

There have been many claims on behalf of Kabbalah water, ranging from its ability to cleanse the lakes of Chernobyl of radiation to its power to cure cancer and AIDS. The principle behind the water is that it is blessed and imbued with spiritual energy, as is holy water from Christian shrines such as Lourdes. This works on the principles demonstrated in the book *Messages from Water* by Masaru Emoto (HADO Publishing). Emoto documented molecular changes in water by freezing droplets of water that had been exposed to different environments, then photographing them through a microscope. Water from clear mountain streams forms regular geometric designs in their crystalline patterns while polluted and stagnant water forms distorted structures.

FAMOUS MODERN KABBALISTS

According to press reports across the world, followers of the Kabbalah Centre include Madonna's husband Guy Ritchie, Demi Moore and husband Ashton Kutcher, Barbra Streisand, Gwyneth Paltrow, Naomi Campbell, Normandie Keith, Sabrina Guinness, Donna Karan, Roseanne Barr and comedienne Sandra Bernhard. Other famous people who have investigated the Kabbalah Centre's teachings include Elizabeth Taylor, Michael Jackson, Courtney Love, Jerry Hall, Mick Jagger, Winona Ryder, Monica Lewinsky, Sarah Ferguson, Britney Spears, Lindsay Lohan and Paris Hilton. David and Victoria Beckham have both been shown on television wearing the centre's trademark red string on their wrist.

LEFT Britney Spears, who was introduced to the Kabbalah Centre by Madonna, says she has now left the movement, preferring to focus on her family. Unconfirmed sources say that she was put off by repeated demands for money. The star's mother, who guided her career for many years, has been publicly hostile to the teachings of the Kabbalah Centre and its encouragement of tithing ten per cent of all income to its work.

The Kabbalah Centre claims that the condition of the water that humans drink determines the quality of the information being transmitted to every atom of their bodies, and that the blessings given to Kabbalah water make it pure and health-giving. The water blessed by the Kabbalah Centre comes from a Canadian bottling plant. The main controversy over Kabbalah water, as with other products from the Kabbalah Centre, is that gullible people may give more credence to claims of healing powers than they merit.

MODERN VERSUS ORTHODOX

KABBALAH HAS ALWAYS BEEN A CROSSOVER PHENOMENON, WITH KABBALISTS TEACHING GENTILES IN THE 3RD, 12TH, 16TH AND 18TH CENTURIES. HOWEVER, THAT TEACHING REQUIRED A COMMITMENT OF SCHOLARSHIP AND DISCIPLINE AND, IF KABBALAH WAS TAUGHT TO WOMEN, IT WAS TAUGHT QUIETLY. THE POPULARITY OF THE KABBALAH CENTRE, ITS PRODUCT LINES AND ITS TEACHING THAT IT IS NOT NECESSARY TO UNDERSTAND HEBREW OR ARAMAIC IN ORDER TO RECEIVE SPIRITUAL INSIGHTS FROM MEDITATING ON THE ZOHAR HAVE ALL MADE IT THE SUBJECT OF DERISION BY "MORE SERIOUS" KABBALISTS, ESPECIALLY THOSE OF THE JEWISH FAITH. THE CENTRE IS THE VERY VISIBLE, EVANGELICAL END OF A VERY BROAD SPECTRUM OF BELIEF AND STUDY BY MODERN KABBALISTS, AND HAS BEEN ACCUSED OF UNIVERSALIZING KABBALAH OUT OF EXISTENCE AND OF MAKING IT A NEW AGE FAD.

RIGHT A religious Jewish Kabbalah scholar reads from the Etz Haym (Tree of Life) holy book during his studies at leading Kabbalist Rabbi Yitzhak Kadouri's synagogue in Jerusalem.

BELOW A pair of Talmudic scholars debate a text in a *yesivah* – an Orthodox Jewish college for advanced study of the Talmud and other works.

The Kabbalah Centre has attracted a great deal of interest, including criticism, for its appeal to modern-day celebrities. It is hard for Orthodox Jews to see a tradition sacred to their own faith taught to gentiles. All non-Jewish Kabbalistic groups – whether or not there is a Jewish head of the group – are disliked by the Orthodox but, because of its fame and popularity, the Kabbalah Centre is the main target.

The centre has some credence in the Jewish world, whether or not its actions are approved, because the head of the Kabbalah Centre is believed

to be an ordained rabbi. However, the fact that it has publicized Kabbalah worldwide means that what was an ancient and revered – if sometimes feared – tradition will now always be associated with a New Age fad. The Orthodox do themselves no favours either with their assertion that Kabbalah may not be taught to women or non-Jews. The world has moved on from such strictures, and the greatest asset of an oral tradition is that it can move with the times.

Although it has become big business with million-pound centres, the financial and personal commitments required by the centre of those who wish to study in depth are not lightweight by any means. Repeated reports in the press refer to four-to-a-bedroom conditions and $35-a-month pocket money accepted by the full-time volunteers.

RABBI YITZHAK KADOURI

The most famous non-celebrity Kabbalist of recent days was Rabbi Yitzhak Kadouri, a Sephardi Jew from Iraq and a revered rabbinical sage, who died in 2006 at the age of 106. Rabbi Kaduri was head of the Kabbalists' centre Beit El (Yeshivat HaMekubalim) in Jerusalem, and he went on record to say that non-Jews, and women in particular, were banned from studying Jewish mysticism. He refused to offer Madonna a blessing on her visit to Israel in 2006.

Rabbi Kadouri did not publish any of his own revered Kabbalistic work but did go public with articles criticizing people who engage in "practical Kabbalah", as well as the now popular distribution of Kabbalistic advice or amulets – often for a price – by those of whom he disapproved. Rabbi Kadouri was well known for his own blessings and amulets, always given without requiring payment and to which were attributed recovery from severe illnesses and from both fertility and financial problems.

ABOVE Leading Jewish Kabbalah scholar Rabbi Yitzhak Kadouri sits in his library with a copy of the Zohar. Kadouri, one of the great contemporary spiritual fathers for Kabbalist followers all over the world, died on 28 January 2006, at the age of 106, in Jerusalem. Originally from Iraq, he immigrated to British-mandate Palestine as a child, and after studies at various Jewish seminaries, became a Kabbalist spiritual leader without ever publishing his teachings.

THE FUTURE OF KABBALAH

Today, Kabbalah is practised as a self-help technique in which no knowledge of Hebrew is required in order to meditate on a word and receive healing, and it is a multimillion-dollar business. Kabbalah is also a tool used by witches in a modern world that currently considers magic amusing and is willing to buy ready-made spells to influence events and people. In total contradiction, it is also a complicated and secretive teaching held closely within the heart of certain groups of Orthodox Jews.

The first two situations are situated on the right pillar of the Tree of Life – and in danger of over-balancing and bringing the teaching into total disrepute. The second is situated on the left-hand pillar of the Tree of Life – and in danger of over-balancing by focusing on severity and limitation, and crystallizing a teaching that was always designed to be adaptable. The seeker of Kabbalistic knowledge and wisdom would be best advised to seek the middle column: one where both pillars are balanced and the teaching is structured, disciplined and merciful. Ultimately, Kabbalah is a system of helping God to behold God. When the student has a clear intention and a wish to seek truth, the correct teacher will appear.

LEFT Kabbalah is one of the most controversial spiritual traditions in the world, thanks to the Kabbalah Centre, its promotion of the "red string", and its corporate image. However, real Kabbalah is not a religion, nor concerned with superstition or celebrity. Whether the current cult of "celebrity Kabbalah" will endure or is simply "the passing show" is irrelevant to the deep inner truth of a tradition that may always be misunderstood by the casual observer.

GLOSSARY

Adam Kadmon
Hebrew for primordial man. The image of God of which each member of humanity is a spark. Adam Kadmon is represented in the world of Azilut.

Alchemy
The science of transforming physical matter into gold in the belief that understanding this will help to comprehend the higher worlds.

Asiyyah
The physical world of making.

Ayin
The Transcendent. Absolute nothing.

Ayin Sof
The Absolute All. God the Immanent or the Infinite without End.

Ayin Sof Or
The Endless Light from which came the emanation that began the unfolding of creation.

Azilut
The divine world of fire and pure emanation: the closest world to God.

Beriah
The spiritual world of air and creation, pure spirit and archangels.

Binah
The Sefira of Understanding and Reason.

Cabala
The spelling of Kabbalah adopted by the Christian tradition.

Da'at
A non-Sefira of Knowledge. The Abyss.

Duality
The opposites that make up the Creation: life and death; day and night; up and down; light and dark; good and bad.

Ego
The Yesod (Foundation) of Yezirah (Psyche). The Ego is our persona and dictates how we react to situations.

Four Journeys
The four stages of growth experienced by the human soul on its journey back to Azilut.

Gematria
A system of complex word codes that work on correspondences between the ten Sefirot and the 22 letters of the Hebrew alphabet.

Genesis
The first book of the Torah and the Bible. In the first chapter of Genesis, God creates the universe and Adam and Eve.

Gevurah
The Sefira of Judgement or Discernment.

Gnostic
From the Greek word *gnosis*, or knowledge from personal experience. The people most often referred to as Gnostics are early Christians who looked beyond the Gospels for the truth of Jesus' teachings. Gnosticism usually views the world as an evil place that needs to be redeemed.

Haggadah
A commentary on the Torah.

Hasidim
Ultra-Orthodox Jews. Followers of the Baal Shem Tov.

Hellenic/Hellenistic
Ancient Greek influence.

Hermeticism
A non-Christian tradition of Hellenistic Gnosticism encompassing alchemy, astrology and theosophy.

Hesed
The Sefira of Mercy or Love.

Hod
The Sefira of Reverberation, Thought and Glory.

Hokhmah
The Sefira of Wisdom, Inspiration and Revelation.

Jacob's Ladder
The diagram of the four worlds of Creation, inspired by the design of the Tabernacle. It demonstrates the invisible laws that maintain the cycles of the stars, planets and nature.

Judaism
The religion of the writers and characters of the Old Testament, which forms the basis for both Christianity and Islam. Jews do not follow the New Testament or the Koran.

Kavanah
A prayer or action with sacred intention.

Karma
The principle of the "law of attraction", "what goes around, comes around".

Keter
The Crown of the Tree of Life.

Lurianic Kabbalah
Kabbalah inspired by the 16th-century theory that God made a mistake during creation.

Merkabah
The object of Merkabah mysticism is one of inner revelation: to recreate the ecstatic vision of ascending to the higher worlds, which the Prophet Ezekiel experienced (Book of Ezekiel).

Malkhut
The lowest Sefira, called the Kingdom.

Menorah
The menorah is one of the oldest symbols of Jewish faith and a model for the Tree of Life. The Torah states that God revealed the design for the seven-branched candelabrum to Moses.

Messiah
The promised deliverer of the Jewish nation prophesied in the Hebrew Bible. The perfect incarnate man at Keter of Yezirah.

Metatron
The great archangel of the presence at Keter of Beriah. Said to be the first fully perfected human being, Enoch.

Midrash
A commentary on the Torah.

Mysticism
The practice of experiencing the divine through intuition, insight or direct knowledge of God. Mystics search for truth beyond general reality or written texts.

Neoplatonism
A philosophical system developed in Alexandria, Egypt, in the 3rd century CE by the philosopher Plotinus and his successors. It is an extension of the teachings of Plato mixed with mystical Judaic and Christian beliefs.

Nezach
The Sefira of Eternity or Repeating.

Occult
Secret, magical and sacred practices, directed towards the supernatural, that are revealed only to those prepared to understand their significance and be initiated into their mysteries.

Orthodox
Adhering to the accepted, traditional version of a faith or belief.

Orthodox Jew
A Jew who follows all 613 laws in the Torah.

Qabalah
The spelling of Kabbalah adopted by the magical tradition.

Reincarnation
The principle of repeating lives in order to perfect the soul.

Sandalphon
The archangel at Malkhut of Beriah.

Sefira/Sefirot
Lights, vessels, faces of the Ten Divine Emanations. Sefira is singular and Sefirot is plural.

Shekhinah
The Divine Presence in Malkhut of Azilut and below. Regarded as the feminine aspect of God.

School of the Soul
A specific group of Kabbalists, representing a particular aspect of the teaching.

Tabernacle
The moveable place of worship for the Israelites in the wilderness. Model for Jacob's Ladder.

Talmud
1st-century commentary on the Torah.

Transmigration
The principle of a soul passing into another body after death.

Tiferet
The Sefira of Beauty at the centre of the Tree of Life.

Tikun
A conscious amendment to cosmic imbalances.

Torah
The first five books of the Hebrew Bible containing the law of the Israelites.

Tree of Life
A visual rendering of the ten Sefirot, the Tree of Life is the seminal diagram of Kabbalah, which is modelled on the menorah.

Yesod
The Sefira of Foundation and the Ego.

Yezirah
The psychological world of emotions, the soul and angels.

Zimzum
The contraction within the Godhead to allow existence to come into being.

INDEX

FURTHER READING

BIBLIOGRAPHY

The Bible (King James Version)

Berg, Michael

The Way (John Wiley & Sons, 2002)

Cohen, A. (Dr)

Everyman's Talmud (J. M. Dent & Sons Ltd, 1995)

Cordovero, Moses

Tomer Devorah (public domain)

Halevi, Z'ev ben Shimon

A Kabbalistic Universe (Kabbalah Society, 1992)

Tree of Life (Kabbalah Society, 2000)

Way of Kabbalah (Kabbalah Society, 2000)

Jayanti, Amber

Principles of the Qabalah (Thorsons, 1999)

Kaplan, Aryeh (ed.)

Sefer Yetzirah (Weisen, 1997)

Parfitt, Will

Elements of the Qabalah (Element, 1997)

Regardie, Israel

The Middle Pillar (Llewellyn, 2002)

Roland, Paul

Kabbalah (Piatkus, 1999)

Scholem, Gershom

Major Trends in Jewish Mysticism (Schocken Books, 1995)

Tishby, Isaiah and Goldstein, David

The Wisdom of the Zohar (Littman Library of Jewish Civilization, 1997)

WEBSITES OF INTEREST

www.kabbalahsociety.org

Website of the Toledano Tradition

www.kabbalah.com

Website of the Kabbalah Centre with daily updates and articles

www.digital-brilliance.com/kab/deborah/deborah.htm

Website with the text of Tomer Devorah by Moses Cordovero

www.kabbalah.org

Jason Schulman's website, A Society of Souls

www.treeofsapphires.com

RECOMMENDED BOOKS

Fortune, Dion

The Training and Work of an Initiate (Weiser, 2000)

Gillespie, Gerald

Kabbalah's Twelve Step Spiritual Method to End Your Addiction (Spi Books, 1997)

Goddard, David

The Sacred Magic of the Angels (Weiser, 1999)

Tower of Alchemy (Weiser, 1996)

The Tree of Sapphires (Weiser, 2004)

Halevi, Z'ev ben Shimon

The Work of the Kabbalist (Weiser, 1993)

School of the Soul (Weiser, 1993)

MacNulty, W. Kirk

Freemasonry (Thames and Hudson, 2006)

Parfitt, Will

Kabbalah for Life (Rider & Co, 2006)

Regardie, Israel

A Garden of Pomegranates (Llewellyn, 1999)

Whitehouse, Maggy

Living Kabbalah (Hamlyn, 2004)